WAITING TO DIE

WAITING TO DIE

LIFE ON DEATH ROW

RICHARD MICHAEL ROSSI

First published Great Britain in 2004 by Vision Paperbacks,
a division of Satin Publications Ltd.
101 Southwark Street
London SE1 0JF
UK
info@visionpaperbacks.co.uk
www.visionpaperbacks.co.uk
Publisher: Sheena Dewan

First published in France by Edition Fayard, 2001

A catalogue record for this book is available from the British Library.

ISBN: 1-904132-52-9

2 4 6 8 10 9 7 5 3 1

Cover and text design by ok?design
Printed and bound in the UK by Mackays of Chatham Ltd,
Chatham, Kent.

to my mother

Further Dedication

This book is dedicated to all the unheard voices on death row, as well as to the continuing efforts to abolish the death penalty by so many wonderful and hard working abolitionists around the world. Hopefully this book will serve as one more tool in the struggle. By describing what goes on within these concrete tombs, the politics of the death penalty and the economics of the prison complex, I hope this book will awaken many more to our plight.

Our biggest weapons against the death penalty are our social conscience and combined voices. Sooner or later, all of us on the row walk through the doorway never to return. Don't allow the efforts of those campaigning against the death penalty to go in vain. Use this book to help in the fight for abolition until it's won.

Contents

Acknowledgments

I wish to thank Earl and Donna Evleth for their support and help editing the French edition of this book. They did a terrific job.

And I wish to thank my dear friend, John A. Pizer, for his editing of the revised and updated English language edition of my book.

Also to be thanked for their support along the way are Dale Baich, Brian Crowther, Trish Bracey, Jack and Felice Cohen-Joppa, LifeLines UK and Ireland, Jan Arriens, Tracy Lamourie and Dave Parkinson of CCADP (Canadian Coalition against Death Penalty), Karen Luderer, Rick Burdick, Hugo Boniche, Lisa Eiger, Ada Berrios, Jennifer Smith, Claudia Whitman and Laird Carlson of Cell Door, Anna Lisa Prevacini, and all my pen pals around the world.

My Friend Richard Rossi — An Appreciation

Almost ten years ago, in April 1994, I received a request from death row, in Arizona, for a pen pal. I responded, being a long-time Amnesty activist, a member of LifeLines and a lifelong abolitionist. Now, at this juncture in the spring of 2004, I have the indescribably difficult task of saying in a few words what Richie has come to mean to me and to my partner Tricia. Time is running out for our beloved friend. The state of Arizona will assuredly kill him in the not too distant future.

Hundreds of letters and cards have passed between the three of us. Five times Tricia and I have made the long trip to Arizona, where the Blue Mist Motel in Florence, opposite to the prison, has become almost a second home. Audio cassettes have been exchanged, examples of Richie's artwork hang in my home, and I have all of his many articles and poems. Every single letter and card he has sent is meticulously filed.

There are remarkable individuals who have the capacity to endure unimaginable privations, like the Tibetan Buddhist monk, Palden Gyatso, who suffered 33 years of incarceration under the Chinese occupiers of his country, and the more famous Nelson Mandela, who was imprisoned by the apartheid regime in South Africa for almost 30 years. While Richie has survived over two decades on death row, I have to express astonishment that he has not been utterly destroyed as a human being. Not only has he survived, he has retained his curiosity about "life on the outside," his keen sense of humor and his innate humanity. He is a truly caring person. Inevitably he has suffered bouts of depression, but he has not allowed the appalling conditions on the row to destroy his humanity or his individuality. I cannot understand how any human being can endure such privations for so long and remain whole. For death row is a torturous hell.

Almost 20 years ago Richie committed a terrible crime, for which severe punishment was merited. Yet I am strongly persuaded that, without in the least condoning heinous crimes, society must allow for change and growth. Most human beings are redeemable, but the death penalty is irrevocable. Capital punishment is an abomination. It is the ultimate in cruel, inhuman and degrading punishment. There should be no place for it in any society calling itself civilized.

Read Richie's graphic account of his long years on death row and try to comprehend the sheer wrongness of such ways of dealing with serious crime. There are other, better ways.

Brian Crowther
USA Death Penalty Coordinator,
Amnesty International UK,
and LifeLines activist

Foreword

Richard Rossi has been on death row for 20 years. At the time of the offence he was 36. He has therefore spent an inordinate time awaiting death, and indeed has spent most of his adult life on death row.

In that sense his story is not atypical. What is atypical is that, as an accountant, he was an educated man with some financial resources. Also unusually, he admits his guilt: for understandable reasons, the majority of prisoners on death row claim they are innocent or that they never intended the killing to take place. Richard Rossi has faced his offence head-on.

I have been corresponding with Richard for the past five years. Over the years he has been a prolific contributor of articles to *The Wing of Friendship*, the quarterly journal of the UK-based organization LifeLines, whose members write to prisoners on death row in the US. I was seeking his permission to use some of his material in a revised edition of *Welcome to Hell*, a collection of extracts from prisoners' letters and articles.

Since then he has become something of a brother. There is a great mutual respect and affection. Through his letters and writings I have seen evidence of a man who has done all that he can to maintain his inner integrity and indeed to grow as a person in the worst of all possible circumstances. I have seen him rise above indignity after indignity; I have seen him all but broken by legal defeats, but never quite giving up hope or losing determination. Above all, I have seen him retain his faith in humanity.

Some would say that when he committed his crime he violated any claim to humanity and forfeited any right to continue participating in society, and indeed to existence. What the correspondence reveals, however, is that an extraordinary number of people on death row look deep inside themselves and blossom against the odds. Richard is a notable example.

Richard wrote the book in the course of our correspondence. It is a devastating indictment of the death penalty and the way in which it is administered in the US today, written from the inside. It carries the authority of one who, from personal experience, knows what he is talking about, but who never allows emotion to carry the day; the facts speak for themselves.

Here, then, is an account from someone who has spent longer under sentence of death than almost anyone else in human history.

Jan Arriens
Founder of LifeLines

Introduction

Since I am in prison, over the years I have learned the ropes, the ins and outs of prison life. I have devoted my time to developing friendships with numerous people in the outside world, as well as to developing my writing skills. I write articles about prison conditions, anecdotes and poems. These essays are published in many anti-death penalty newsletters, which are produced and read by a tight-knit group of abolitionists. People who have read my articles sometimes write to me. Most of these people are outside the United States. They are always amazed at the answers to their inquiries about life on death row and the accompanying hardships and cruelties we endure. They find it truly an alien world; they are outraged by what they hear.

These people have been very supportive in encouraging me to write this book. They feel that the truth about death row and the death penalty can be a strong tool in the fight to abolish capital punishment. They realize that the United States is the only democratic society that executes its citizens. Abolitionists also want to expose the gulags called "control unit prisons."

I intend this book to be a primer, a textbook depiction of this bizarre world. All of my material is 100 percent accurate and honest, with no exaggeration. After all, one cannot make up stuff like this.

Welcome to prison!

Richard Michael Rossi #50337
P.O. Box 3400
Florence, AZ 85232
USA

Weeds

Weeds,
That's what we are.

Most people stomp them with their boots
Or pull them out by their roots.
Some mow them down,
Others pour poison around.

Not in my neighborhood, not in my yard,
They are very careful not to drop their guard.
And fear we will never go away,
So they kill us one special day.

Politicians can't win unless they agree,
That weeds have no value, they must punish me.
The Governor could free us with a stroke of his pen,
But he fears this will land him in the lion's den.
Behind these walls are thousands of weeds,
We are here because of our terrible deeds.
Weeds are young, weeds are old, some short, some tall,
Loved ones visit from time to time,
They're the only ones who care at all.

Weeds are like strangers in their own land,
Just waiting for someone to extend us a hand.
How many years will it take you to see,
That some weeds have value and should grow free?

Richard Rossi—October 1994

CHAPTER 1

FROM THE BEGINNING

My name is Richard Michael Rossi. I am a convicted murderer on death row at the Arizona State Prison at Florence. I was convicted of killing a man with whom I had an argument over a stolen typewriter that I was attempting to sell. I was selling the typewriter to get money to buy cocaine, a drug that I was addicted to. I became addicted to cocaine in the late 1970s, when I was living in Brooklyn, New York, where I was born and raised. When I finally realized I was destroying my life with drugs, I decided to clean up, so I moved to Phoenix, Arizona where my parents had retired. In Phoenix I resumed my career as an accountant and did not use any cocaine for the next three years. But my relationship with my live-in girlfriend was not going well. She was an alcoholic and a drug abuser herself. Her fears and insecurities put great strain on me. The pressure built up to an unbearable, explosive point. Finally on my birthday, June 30, 1983, when a friend offered me some cocaine, I was so miserable that I convinced myself that I deserved some relief. That was the biggest mistake of my life. In two months I used all of my savings to buy cocaine. I resorted to selling my personal property as well as a stolen typewriter.

On August 29, 1983, I went to a man's house to sell him this stolen typewriter. I had been up over 24 hours straight, shooting coke into my veins. I was on a binge and needed more cocaine. I was paranoid and jittery. My mind was telling me that things were happening around me that were not. When I brought the typewriter to the man, he cut the price he had previously agreed to. He saw the terrible condition I was in and felt he could put one over on me. He said that if I did not take his price, he would phone the police and inform them that I was selling stolen property. When he said he had a gun, I became more nervous and paranoid. When he went into another room to get the money, I imagined that I was hearing a conversation. I feared he was on the phone to the police. I burst into the room. He began running toward a drawer. I thought that he was going for his gun, so I pulled out my own gun and fired three quick shots. He died instantly. I took the money, and as I was leaving a neighbor who had heard the shots came running in. I panicked, shot the neighbor twice and ran out. Fortunately, the neighbor did not die.

I was later arrested and convicted of first-degree murder. I denied my guilt throughout the trial and for a year or two afterward. Finally I realized what a terrible thing I had done and accepted responsibility for my actions. How easy it is to pull the trigger of a gun and rob someone of their life. Life is sacred. It cannot be replaced no matter how hard one wishes or how remorseful one is. In my case, it was all because of drug addiction and paranoia, a sickness of the mind and body. The craving was so strong that it overcame my ability to distinguish right from wrong.

* * *

In the 20 years that I have been on death row, not a day goes by that I do not reflect on what I have done. It haunts me to this day. It is a pain I will carry to my grave. The fact that I took the money when I left the scene qualified me for the death penalty. The law states that if in the commission of a felony (such as robbery) someone dies, you have committed capital murder and you can receive the death penalty. Although it is widely believed that only the most heinous and depraved criminals such as serial killers and child murderers, the "worst of the worst," receive the death penalty, that is false. Most of those on death row did not commit a particularly heinous crime. Their crimes were much like mine. However, the laws can be manipulated so that any first-degree murder can be punished with the death penalty. For the overzealous and promotion-oriented prosecutor the death penalty is a means of advancement. The more death penalty convictions they obtain, the higher up the ladder of success they climb.

Most perpetrators who commit murder do not appreciate the gravity of the act at the time, for numerous reasons. Drugs, passion, economics, anger, ignorance, fear, boldness and arrogance all play a role. But once the individual is isolated from the circumstances which contributed to the act and is sitting on death row, the senselessness of their crime becomes clear.

Death row is unlike any other place in the prison system. Not just in the physical constraints, but in the penal philosophy and management of death row prisoners. The pressures of a general population prisoner can be multiplied tenfold and still not equal the pressures for a death row prisoner. It is an advanced, accelerated form of punishment.

I was born on June 30, 1947 in Brooklyn, New York. I was an only child. My parents were hard-working people without much formal education. My father was a cook in the army during World War II and when he came home from service he got into the restaurant business. He opened a diner. When that failed, he opened another diner. He was not very successful and accumulated large debts. My mother worked with him in the diner. When I was five years old, my father walked out on my mother and me. He left tremendous debts for my mother, which her pride compelled her to work many years to pay off.

When my father was around, he used his belt whenever he felt I was out of line or when he just was not in the mood to deal with a child. Toward the end he became more and more violent with me. Because we were poor, I rarely got any toys to play with. For one of my birthdays I received a small plastic guitar. I was crazy about it. I would pluck the strings day and night. I remember one day as we were in the car going someplace, I was in the back seat with my guitar. I was strumming it and that annoyed my father. He told me to stop. A few minutes later I started again, and quicker than you could blink an eye he swung around and hit me so hard across the face that I wound up on the opposite side of the car. Then he took the guitar and threw it out the window. It was run over by another car. I was traumatized. After that I got beaten each and every day for something.

A few years after my father left my mother remarried. My stepfather was a quiet type of person and so the responsibility of being the disciplinarian fell to her. She was a stern disciplinarian.

She had iron hands and used them frequently and unmercifully. I did not have to do something wrong to get hit. She gave me preemptive beatings. She beat me so often that her hands hurt. Then she used her slipper to hit me. This hurt me more and her less. She would grab me by the arm or hand and pull me toward her, then she would smack me with the slipper until I was red or black and blue. Eventually I would break away and run to the next room. Then she would throw the slipper at me and usually hit me in the back. I was so afraid of her that when she would order me to return the slipper, I would pick it up and bring it back to her! Then she would grab my arm and start beating me again. Finally I realized that it was not to my advantage to return the slipper to her when she told me to. But still I felt guilty because I was disobeying her.

Since I had no brothers or sisters, there was no one I could talk to about the beatings. The trauma escalated. I grew to hate my sad, childhood life. I felt like I was an adult inside a child's body. My thoughts were ahead of my years, but I knew I could not break free of my parents. There was little love and lots of aggression. I was trapped and hopelessly stuck in my situation.

My mother substituted food for love. As a result, I became obese as a child. I was five feet tall and weighed 220 pounds. To get pants for school, we had to go to a big man's store because the clothes in the regular stores were too small for me to fit into. The pants had no style and were the clothes of an old man. At school the other kids had pants that were in style and in all cuts and colors. Often the seams of my pants would burst open in school when I bent over and my body would stick out. The other kids laughed. This cruel teasing hurt a lot.

I became lonelier and hated that as well. I would go to the playground directly across the street from our house, but no one would pick me for their baseball or stickball teams. On top of that, they made fun of me. I would sit on the sidelines and just watch the others play ball. Then I would go home to my room and cry for hours. This went on throughout my childhood.

Growing up in the 1950s was nothing like it is today. There were no video games, no gadgets, no computers. We had baseball as the most popular sport and we had the neighborhood movie theater. I got 50 cents a week allowance and I spent it on the movies. It cost 25 cents to get in and with the other 25 cents I could buy five candy bars. Westerns were all the rage at that time—Hopalong Cassidy, Roy Rogers, Gene Autry and the Lone Ranger. We all had cap pistols and everything was "bang, bang, shoot em' up." That was when I became enamored with guns. I wanted a real one.

I lived a mile or two from Ebbets Field in Brooklyn, the home of the Brooklyn Dodgers baseball team. This was before the television sports channels. In Brooklyn, baseball was the major event. Baseball was the glue that held everything together. If you came from Brooklyn, you had to be a Dodgers fan. Pee Wee Reese was my hero. He played shortstop for the Dodgers from 1940 to 1958. My first baseball glove was a Pee Wee Reese model.

Once a month, our church received a group pass to allow 25 kids in to see the Dodgers play on Saturday afternoons. The second time I was to go with the group to the game, I arrived at the church too late and the group had left without me. I ran to the stadium but had no luck finding them. I stood there and cried. A man from another group saw me crying and asked what was wrong. I told him I had missed my group and was not going to get in to see the game. He said that I could go in with his group. I was overwhelmed with happiness.

It did not take me long to realize that I might be able to walk up to the stadium each Saturday and start crying until someone offered to take me in to the ballpark with their group. Using this method, I seldom missed a ballgame. When I could not get in, I would lie down on the pavement opposite the large steel doors where the machinery was brought in to maintain the field. I could see under the door and watch Carl Furillo in right field. I waited for home runs to be hit out of the park so that I could run after them. I did not have any money to buy hot dogs or sodas, but I was happy just the same. I brought half a loaf of Italian bread with me and nibbled on it throughout the game. It was just great to watch the teams or to listen to the boos directed at the umpires. To be a Brooklyn Dodgers fan was the best thing in the world!

Besides getting into baseball games I tried other bits of childish chicanery. At elementary school the teacher would assign various students as monitors. The monitors did specific tasks like cleaning the blackboards or opening and closing the windows. My job was to be the milk and cookie monitor. Each day the pupils would purchase a carton of milk and some biscuits for the morning milk and cookie break. The milks were three cents and the cookies were one cent each. Since I only got five cents a day I could only buy two cookies, and I loved those cookies. Each day the teacher made a list of how many milks and how many boxes of biscuits she needed and I was sent to the basement storeroom to pick up the items and carry them back to class. One day as I was carrying a crate of milk and two boxes of Chocolate Graham Crackers up the stairs I stumbled and one of the boxes of biscuits tumbled down. I went back, picked up the box and continued on my way. Later when the teacher reached the bottom of the box of crackers she noticed lots of broken pieces. Since she could not put them together and sell them to the children, she told me that since I was the cookie monitor, I could have all of the broken pieces and the crumbs. I was in "pig heaven!" I learned quickly that if once or twice a week a box of biscuits "accidentally" fell down the stairs, I would be a happy lad.

When I was about nine or ten, I had a bad accident. I was playing "Cowboys and Indians" with a cousin of mine in the garage. I ran out to shoot some Indians while my cousin was lowering the overhead garage door. The corner of the door hit me squarely on the head and knocked me out. When I came around I was in Kings County Hospital. The doctors put 17 stitches into my head. Before they could do this, they had to inject an anesthetic directly into the skull around the perimeter of the opening. During the process, the needle broke off twice and they had to use heavy-duty pliers to pull the broken piece out of my head. I was awake through the entire process. I have never really been the same since. I have been told that I have organic brain damage. However I cannot tell whether I am different from others because I don't know how other people's brains work. All I can say is that I see things as I see them.

About this time too, it was realized that something had to be done about my weight. My mother, also obese, used to go to her family doctor for diet pills. In the 1950s little was known about the addictive effects of amphetamines.

Many people took diet pills. They were a wonder drug, the darling of the housewife. My mother started giving me some of her diet pills to help me lose weight. I immediately started "buzzing" around the house, cleaning everything in sight. I was high, but I did not know it. I had a heavy sense of euphoria. I also started losing some weight, so my mother took me to the doctor when she went and asked him to put me on the pills. He did. This went on for years. As I began to lose weight, the dosages had to be increased. I did not realize until I later that it was the amphetamines that started me onto cocaine and speed. I had substituted one drug for another. Between the hit on my head and the pills, I was in a world of my own.

Things did not get better for me in my adolescence. Like most teenagers I had acne, but mine was the worst type, cystic acne. My face had more holes and bumps than a golf ball. It was also on my shoulders, back and chest. I had to go to a dermatologist weekly. This went on through junior high school and high school. Obese and with cystic acne, school was no fun. I had no social life and never had any girlfriends. I realized that my life would not begin until I was older, when I could outgrow the acne and slim down.

Despite these handicaps, I did well academically. In high school I was only a C+ student because I had to work after school each day. But when it came to the tests, I did fine. I got one of the highest scores on the Statewide Regents Exam and won a four-year scholarship to college. Since I spent most of my time by myself, I often listened to the news. I was a student of current affairs, and thus I discovered the death penalty. I did not know much about the death penalty except that we were killing people who were convicted of killing others. I followed one particular death row prisoner named Caryl Chessman. He seemed to be constantly living on the edge. He was always hours away from being executed. For years he went from one stay of execution to another. I remember thinking then that for someone to live life locked up in that little cage worrying from day to day, month to month, year to year, must be the hardest and cruelest existence imaginable.

I graduated from Pace College in Manhattan in 1970 with a Bachelor's Degree in Business Administration and Accounting. During those college years I grew to detest what our government was doing to our own people and to others around the world. The 1960s were unique in history. The youth of society were revolting against authority figures and the government. I fitted in well. I did my best to be a hippie and a nonconformist. College taught me how to think. I was suspicious of much of what the government was telling us about Vietnam and other matters at home. As it turned out, we were correct in opposing the war and refusing to believe all the lies that Richard Nixon was telling us. I was involved in many sit-in demonstrations and protest marches, for civil rights as well as against the war. There was a feeling of solidarity in the protest group that was appealing to me. For once I could be part of a group and be accepted. Then came the day when we heard about the National Guard opening fire on the students at Kent State

University. I could not believe that four students who were just exercising their right to protest could be killed in cold blood. It was as if it happened to me. We immediately took to the streets outside the college. Pace is directly across the street from City Hall in Manhattan.

Coincidentally, there was a demonstration by a group of "hard hat" construction workers in front of City Hall. When these big burly guys saw us protesting, they ran across the street with baseball bats and clubs and started assaulting us. We were all injured. The police did not even try to stop the violence. This did not shock me. The police disliked young people who were against our government due to the war. We were communists and traitors to them. It was a day I will never forget. I was injured along with all the others. Some of us had to go to the hospital for our wounds. This event strengthened my resolve against what was going on. I could not just sit back and watch all the injustice. I did not understand why it was okay to kill and injure another race in such an immoral war. Killing was and is wrong. Eventually the troops came home and the war ended and I think now that people look back at the war and see that we protesters had been right.

I got married upon graduation from college. My wife, Lena, also had not had a happy childhood. Her mother died when she was very young and her father brought her and her two sisters up alone. He was abusive and put the girls through a lot of punishment and neglect.

I had never had a love relationship in my adolescence. I only began dating in college. One night I was at a disco in Sheepshead Bay, Brooklyn, when I observed a very pretty young woman having a drink with a female friend. She was about five foot six, with brown hair and a great body. I asked her to dance, and then at the end of the evening I got her phone number and we began dating regularly. Our family backgrounds were similar and we felt simpatico. Our courtship lasted two years before we married.

We both experimented with psychedelic drugs during the period of "flower power." Some called it the "Age of Aquarius," but in reality it was a time to be stoned and stupid. I had got a good job with a large corporation as an accountant, but I was asked to cut my hair. It was a huge decision for me to make because I felt that the long hair symbolized my independence and freedom. I decided to stand on my principles and refused to cut my hair. I was fired.

My wife and I decided to start a small business. Without much money it was difficult. I made some very creative beanbag furniture and we opened a combination gift and head shop. Unfortunately I did not realize the importance of location. The local neighborhood traffic could not support the store. There was a grocery store next door to the gift shop whose owner was retiring. It was an old store, but I thought I could modernize it. We borrowed the money for the business from one of Lena's relatives.

It was hard work, but I took to it. The problem was that our lives began to revolve around too many hours of work. We were both doing drugs. I was taking diet pills again to give me the pep and ability to work 12 to14 hours a day, seven days a week. After work I would go home and take a Quaalude or smoke a joint to mellow out. Drugs became a major part of my life. After a while, Lena told me she wanted to go to the West Coast and live in a commune where one of her cousins lived. I knew she was tired of the daily grind, but I only learned later that the real reason she wanted out of the marriage was because she had fallen in love with someone else. The "other person" was another woman. At the time I only saw how exhausted I was each day from the work, and I could not blame her for wanting out of the routine and relationship. I did not resist our breakup.

I was left with an ailing gift shop and a grocery store that needed lots of work. I closed the gift shop and concentrated on the grocery store. All the starch was coming out of me. When Lena left, I felt rejected and alone once again. But I kept on going, working endless hours, and the store was doing well. Things were finally paying off. I was able to modernize the store as I had envisioned. However, there was a major emotional void in my life again.

After a few years, I successfully sold the business. I was afraid to get married again for fear of failing once more. I could not live with that. With the money from the business I traveled to North America, Mexico and Europe, living a fast but empty life. By 1980 I was hooked on drugs again and in debt. I owed everyone, including the loan sharks. I moved to Arizona where my parents had retired. I stopped the drugs cold turkey and went straight for the first time in many years. I did not do any amphetamines or cocaine for three years and I worked as an accountant again.

I had been living with a woman before moving to Arizona. She moved there with me. This was a big mistake. Life was very lonely for her during the days while I was at work. She was stuck in the apartment all day long because she could not drive and did not have a job. She secretly started drinking while I was at work. When I finally realized what was going on, it was too much to deal with. I tried to get her to go back to New York and live with her mother. She would not. She even threatened to tell the loan sharks and others where I was living if I forced her to leave. I could not call her bluff. Too much was at stake. I was stuck.

During the day while I was at work she would call me numerous times to check on me. She was convinced I was having an affair with another woman in the office. I had not cheated on her. One day I had had enough and told her to move out. In response, she cut her wrists. The police and an ambulance came to our apartment. It was recorded as a domestic disturbance. I did not learn until much later, when I was sitting in a cell in the county jail reading the police reports on my case, that the domestic dispute report was part of the record. My girlfriend had told the police when they asked her why she had slit her wrists that I forced her to take drugs.

A short time after the wrist-slitting incident it was my birthday. A friend offered me some cocaine in the spirit of the party. All the previous times I had refused. However, this time I felt I needed to get high to relieve the pressure I was going through. I had not done any in over three years, but "once a junkie, always a junkie!" It was all down hill from that point on.

When cocaine controls you, you become very paranoid. You see things that are not there and hear things that are not being said. All you want to do is to consume more and more of the drug. I did not snort it, I either smoked it as freebase (crack) or shot it into my veins. I lived for the rush. I stayed up days on end doing the drug. I thought everything was just fine, but of course it wasn't. In the two months leading up to my crime I went through thousands of dollars, all of my savings, doing endless amounts of coke.

When it was all over, I found myself in the county jail awaiting trial for first-degree murder. It would be easy to blame others for what I did, but that is not the reality. Like most people in my position, I went into denial. It took me a few years to come to accept my responsibility for my actions instead of blaming it on circumstances or the people in my life.

Like most people in jail for the first time I knew little about the legal system. It is easy to make wrong decisions about your case, to be misled and get yourself into trouble real fast. If you are without funds a public defender is appointed. If there is a conflict with that, a private attorney is appointed from a list of contract attorneys who work for the county. The state has seemingly unlimited resources to use against the defendant but the appointed attorney has a very small allowance to work with. He must ask the judge for the appointment of experts and investigators and is usually given a small budget for these purposes. The balance is not in the defendant's favor at all.

Before my case was turned over to a contract attorney because of a conflict, a public defender was assigned to me. I saw him twice in six months. Public defenders are overworked and underpaid. Their caseloads are just too large to handle, so they take as many shortcuts as they can.

The second time he came to see me he had a plea bargain offer from the state. He told me that if I pled guilty to the charges, I would get a life sentence for the murder, which is 25 years to life. Along with that I would get 21 years for the attempted murder and the burglary charge would be dropped. The problem was that the sentences would be served consecutively, which meant a total sentence of 46 years. With time off for good behavior I was looking at a minimum of 39 years. I was 36 at the time, so I would not get the opportunity to be paroled until I was at least 75 years old. I could not accept that. I asked him if the state would offer to run the charges concurrently (at the same time). He told me no. He only took 15 minutes to explain the details of the deal that was offered. I commented to him that if the state was willing to offer me this reduced plea bargain, didn't it mean that they had a weak case? He told me they had a lot of circumstantial evidence against me and if I did not take the deal the state would seek the death penalty.

So should I take the deal? Not having been in trouble before, I could not believe how fast my life was being sent down the river! I had to decide there and then. I could not think about it over night. I was afraid to accept such a long sentence without even a chance to go before a jury of my peers. I saw no choice but to go to trial. The other alternative was to die in prison. I would take my chances on my guaranteed right to a trial as stated in the Constitution.

The state did indeed decide to seek the death penalty. They won.

As I look back at what went on during the trial I understand better now how the law works and what should have been done. The problems are appalling. A defendant is assigned very poor representation from the beginning of the trial. This results in numerous mistakes. At the time of the trial you do not know what is going on because you do not know about trial law, or law in general. For the next five to ten years you must try to undo the mistakes that took place during the trial and the direct appeal. The direct appeal is a first, automatic appeal limited to the issues raised during the trial. If you fail to raise certain issues in the direct appeal you are barred from ever raising them.

Indigent representation is another major problem that is at a crisis point. It is true that the US Supreme Court recognizes that indigent defendants are guaranteed legal counsel and equal protection under the law, but the standards of the representation vary from state to state. There is no nationwide guarantee of the quality of representation.

A case called Gideon v. Wainwright (83 SCt 792, 372 US 335) created the principle of indigent representation in 1963. Gideon was an uneducated white man in Florida who was arrested for a crime and did not have any money for legal defense. He was convicted and sent to prison without representation. In those days there was no right to a court-appointed attorney. In prison, Gideon taught himself the law in the law library and filed writ after writ until he got it right and eventually won his freedom. In the process of gaining his freedom, he set a precedent, a landmark decision guaranteeing the right of all defendants to a court-appointed attorney if they cannot afford one.

There are contract attorneys all over this country who work for the county and take huge caseloads for ridiculously low pay. For example, recently one attorney in Alabama took a full-time contract for a yearly fee of $13,000. Another attorney in Georgia has been paid $24,000 per year for a few years now.

His caseload for the previous year was approximately 400 cases. All but three of them were pled out in a plea bargain deal, and only three cases had actual motions entered on their behalf. The contract attorney just tells his clients that the only chance they have is to bargain for a lower crime because going to trial would certainly mean losing and doing a longer sentence. What can a poor person do when faced with such a situation? Can you really believe that such defense attorneys are acting in the best interest of their clients? Or are such defenders actually nothing more than surrogate prosecutors? The reason you rarely see rich people in prison is not because they are less guilty, it is because they can afford proper legal representation. Poor people cannot afford the "dream team" defense of celebrities like O.J. Simpson and others. Many trials can be avoided by restitution or enrollment in rehabilitation programs, but these options take money from the defendant and so that door is closed to the poor. Once a poor person enters the system, there is little hope of not serving time. The rich can afford the best justice money can buy and the poor go to jail. This is not equal justice under the law, guaranteed by the Constitution. The playing field is definitely uneven. Rich people do not go to death row.

It gets even more complicated when you are medicated during your trial. My craving for drugs was never ending. The whole day and night before my crime I was shooting cocaine so I went through withdrawal in the county jail. I reported to the medical staff that I was on various types of anti-psychotic medications while on the streets and that I needed to have them dispensed to me immediately. They did this. Even the psychiatrists ordered heavy medications for me. The problem came when I was at trial. I was being sedated with large doses of Thorazine, Artane and Elavil. I did not have a clue about what was going on in my defense. I could not participate, which is, or should be, a cornerstone in one's defense. The law states that you must know what is going on in order to have a fair trial. I was there in body, but I was a mental zombie.

At the time, the psychiatrists did not know the effect of allowing a person to be medicated this way and how it violated the law. They do know now. The psychiatrists admitted it on the stand at my resentencing hearing. However, the courts allow the state to claim that this argument should have been brought up in an earlier appeal. Thus you are "precluded" from raising the issue. These days more people are being executed due to preclusion than any other issue. If your attorney does not bring up an issue in a timely manner, the issue is lost forever. No matter how important it is. The prisoner is responsible for the actions of his attorney. That is just one of the mistakes that happened to me.

About six years ago my current attorney, Dale, asked me some questions about my ex-wife Lena. He was preparing affidavits for our Habeas Corpus Petition (an application to the court asking the court to release possession of the person regarding violations of constitutional rights). I told him I had not seen or heard from her in close to 30 years. He asked if I would object to having his private investigator try to locate her. I told him I did not mind if he thought this would help the case. He said that an affidavit from her about my drug consumption when we were married would be helpful. A few weeks later I received a letter from Dale. He said that they had located Lena. She was shocked to hear what had happened to me and said that she would gladly give him an affidavit. Unbelievably Lena was living 60 miles away from me in Tucson, Arizona. After all these years she was a few miles away from me. Dale got together with her and got her affidavit. I wrote a letter to Lena and asked Dale to pass it on to her. A month went by and I heard nothing. I gave Dale another letter for her. I had no idea how she would react to my letters.

I finally received a letter from her and she went into detail about her last 28 years without me. She told me that the reason she left me was because while we were married she fell in love with another woman. When she left me, she went to live with this other woman and she had been a feminist and lesbian ever since. She said that it was not my fault the marriage fell apart. I was breathless. For nearly 30 years I had carried this feeling of guilt around with me because I thought I had failed in marriage. In all of those years I would not allow myself to remarry because I could not bear the pain and suffering if I failed in love again. It is hard to explain the emotions I felt when I found this out. There was relief along with regret. Perhaps the regret was because all these years I ran from serious relationships feeling that I could not make them work. But who could have known?

After a few months of letter writing, Lena put in an application and eventually was approved to visit. The day she came to visit was a very special day. We had two hours to sit and talk. I told her that I would always consider her my family and that I had always loved her. She is now the only part of my old family that is left. I told her I had been miserably lonely all these years on death row. Except for one visit from my Godchild, no one else ever bothered to come to Arizona to visit me. Our meeting brought tears to my eyes.

I have tried to figure out how Lena could be living so close to me and how we could be able to see each other. It staggers my mind. When I told a good friend of mine, Rick, this story he said that for Lena to come and visit me meant there had to have been a lot of love in our relationship. Later in my cell I thought about what Rick had said and I have to agree completely. I know that there is still love, not as husband and wife, but as two caring human beings. I do not know how long she will remain in Tucson, but the time I have been able to spend with her has done me much good.

I had to wonder what would cause an ex-wife, lesbian and feminist, to want to come to see me on death row in the middle of the desert. It certainly has to have something to do with character and compassion as a human being, a capacity for love and life. I was a person who always treated her kindly and loved her, a good person, not the monster that society sees in me today and wants to write off as garbage and kill. This may seem small to most people, but it is a major comfort for me. I have been given the opportunity to go back to the beginning of my adult life and fill in the blanks, the missing pieces. I realize how fortunate I am to have this chance. How could this happen to such a lonely and lost person such as myself on death row? What a gift. It has reinforced my feeling of self worth. That is very important. It is like coming full circle. And best of all, I have a friend who cares about me.

CHAPTER 2

ANOTHER DAY IN PARADISE

When I first came to prison, there were only 5 or 6,000 prisoners behind bars in the entire system in Arizona, now there are 30,000. We used to be treated with some respect. As long as we did not make trouble, things went along fairly smoothly. The guards were decent and the food was edible. We had some rights and privileges. That was before the mean-spirited conservative politicians, both in the administration and in congress, embarked on policies to take away what they considered the "frills" in the prison systems. Governors made a point of ensuring that prisoners were not living in the "lap of luxury." Draconian new measures have made life very difficult for those in prison. Politicians have been campaigning to curb what they see as the "Judicial Activism" practiced by the federal district court judges because they grant relief in prisoner class action law suits regarding unconstitutional conditions in prison. In 1996 the Prison Litigation Reform Act was passed, which allows states to dissolve consent decrees by petitioning the courts. Consent decrees are one of the few ways a prisoner can affect changes in prison abuses: the prisoner sues in state and federal courts—when the defendant (the state) believes it will lose they enter a consent decree, in which they agree to make the remedial changes. Previously, consent decrees remained in effect for many years and the courts monitored progress in making the changes. To dissolve a consent decree the state had to prove that no further relief was necessary. The PLRA changed this by allowing the state to simply file a motion to dissolve, asserting that no further relief is necessary. No proof is required. Prisoners have thus lost all the hard fought gains of the past in prison reform. With no court monitoring, the abuses are repeated. The Antiterrorism Effective Death Penalty Act was also passed in 1996, which severely restricts our habeas corpus rights.

The politicians have succeeded and the results are appalling. Law libraries have been dismantled, access to the courts has suffered. Life for the prisoner is at a level equal to that of the 1940s. No relief is in sight. Parole has effectively been done away with: convicts must serve 85 percent of their sentence. There is no rehabilitation and little education to give the prisoner a chance of employment upon release from prison. Medical services are horrible. Morale is low and frustration is high.

The first part of this chapter will portray the typical life on death row, describing the food, housing and general physical conditions. The second part will explain about the services, religious and medical, that we receive. The third part deals with our relations with the prison administration and explains the policies and rules we live under.

* * *

A typical life

Counts

The day begins at 5 a.m. when the day shift comes on and makes its first "walk" to count heads. When the formal count is taken, if the officer does not see a prisoner breathing or moving he will bang on the front of the cell and wake them up to make sure they are alive. The officers do not do this "welfare check" because they are concerned about our health, but because most of the people who die in prison, whether from natural causes or suicide, do so at night. If they find a dead person, a specific procedure must be followed, and the official count must be reduced by one. If the count does not match their computer printout of the last count, the count will be repeated until the numbers do match. There are five formal counts per day. Informal counts function basically the same, except that no official list is checked. It is just a walk through the pods, cell by cell, to see that someone is in each cell and to make sure that no one is up to mischief.

Why are the living areas called "pods"? Doubtless because the cells are lined up one after another, like "peas in a pod." Our pods have five cells on the first floor and five directly above, thus ten to a pod. There are six pods to the cluster, with a total of sixty cells. Each wing of the prison has two to four clusters. The entire unit of 12 clusters houses 720 prisoners. Each cell can be observed by the control tower officer. If you envision the control tower as the hub of a wheel, then the pods are the spokes jutting out in a radial fashion. Computers and TV monitors allow the tower officer to see all and to electronically open any door.

The rules forbid more than one door to be opened at any one time. An intercom allows him to communicate with any prisoner in any pod. Each cell and the upstairs and downstairs showers have an additional manual locking device. An arrangement similar to a hinge and pin is welded onto both the door and the frame. When the door is closed, a pin is manually dropped through the loops and this prevents the tower guard from accidentally opening a door when a prisoner is not handcuffed.

One night a few years ago, I was awakened by the noise of the officers' walkie-talkies. It was about 3:30 a.m. I looked out of my cell front and saw an officer trying to wake a friend of mine a few cells away. The prisoner was seated on the toilet. The officer tried everything to get a response from the prisoner, including giving him a direct order to answer up. If you disobey a direct order, you are given a disciplinary writeup. My friend, Al, was not phased even by this very serious threat. The officer left the pod. About 20 minutes later he returned with his supervisor and three other officers. They once again tried to get a response from Al. He did not move an inch or say a word. Again they left. About 15 minutes later a dozen police entered the pod in full battle gear—vests, helmets and shields. All the lights in the pod were turned on high including those inside the cells. There was an officer with a video camera to record the events, the usual practice when they forcibly evict someone from a cell.

With their batons, the police rapped on the cell front very loudly. Still no movement. After a few minutes of this din, someone finally concluded that Al might be dead. They would have to enter his cell to check this out. But what if he was fooling and jumped up and attacked them? They arranged themselves in formation outside the cell and the supervisor radioed to the control room for the door to be opened. A dozen officers rushed into the cell and circled the toilet. Al was indeed dead. Now there was no rush. It took about an hour to remove Al from the toilet, put him on a stretcher and take him away. The scene was documented with videotape and Polaroid pictures. About an hour later, a full squad of officers returned to the pod. One by one we were all removed from our cells to the outside exercise area and our cells were torn apart by a massive search. Since they did not know at that time what the official cause of death was, they needed to make sure that Al had not been killed with a weapon or poisoned. They found nothing. A subsequent autopsy confirmed that Al had had a massive heart attack.

Feeding

At approximately 3:30 a.m. the food carts are rolled into the area outside the cells by the night shift. At 4:30 a.m. the pods are fed. Two officers wearing flak jackets and eye goggles enter the pod with the food trays. They make sure that each cell door has its additional manual locking pin securely in place.

As they approach the cells, one officer carries a stack of food trays and the other has a key in his hand. The key is to unlock the food tray slot, a six by twelve inch solid steel door with an outside lock on it. When the door is unlocked it provides a platform for the food tray to sit on. To insure that you are awake when they come into the pod to feed, they slam the doors of the food carts when they take the food trays out, bang the lids of the trays and make a thorough racket. No one can sleep through the noise.

Before the officer will open the food slot to put the tray in, he will make sure the prisoner is sitting on his bunk at the back of the cell. If the prisoner is not sitting there, he will not be fed. We cannot be standing up or be anywhere near the front of the cell. Once the tray slot door is opened, the trays are placed on the ledge and the officers step away. Then one will say "okay." That is the cue to approach the cell front and take the food tray. After stepping back to the bunk at the back of the cell, the officer slams the tray slot closed. It is like slamming the door on an animal's cage in the zoo.

Why feed like this? Because we are considered so dangerous that we cannot be allowed to come out of our cages and assemble in a dining hall. It is amazing to observe how conditioned we become after being treated like this for years on end. Occasionally, when the meals are delayed by as little as a few minutes, our bodies and minds go through changes. We start worrying if we are to be fed at all, or if our entire world is coming to an end. Perhaps World War III has started and orders have been given to kill the prisoners. Maybe the death squads are coming.

With each tray in the morning we are given a packet that contains two plastic "sporks" (spoon/fork), salt and pepper, a tea bag, a packet of instant coffee and a packet of fruit drink mix. These packets make eight ounces of beverage. Since we do not receive hot water or ice, we must mix these drinks with the tap water from the sink.

The return of the empty food trays after meals is a security matter. If for some reason a prisoner decides not to give back his empty plastic food tray, the officer demands the tray. He gives a direct order to return the tray. If the prisoner still refuses, he goes outside of the pod and calls his supervisor on his radio. The supervisor comes to the cell and asks for the tray. If the prisoner refuses again, the supervisor assembles the goon squad. About a dozen officers will return in full battle gear. Someone videotapes it all. The prisoner is given one last chance to give up the tray. If he still refuses, they begin spraying him with mace or pepper spray. When he succumbs to the gas, they will open the cell door and rush him. Sometimes, instead of the gas, they bring the German shepherd attack dog to the cell. When the door is opened, the dog attacks the prisoner followed by the police. Then he is beaten, dragged outside, stripped of all his clothes, and placed in a holding cell, a small concrete room measuring about four and a half feet square. It is too small to permit a person to physically stretch out. The recalcitrant prisoner is kept there from one to three days. The psychiatrist is summoned to speak to him. While he is in this holding cell, he is given no blanket. He is fed a sack lunch three times a day: four slices of bread with two paper-thin slices of luncheon meat, an apple or an orange. His property is removed from his old cell and taken to the property room to be searched and abused. Afterward he is given a disciplinary write up and either returned to his old cell or put in a more secure cell. He loses his privileges for 30 days. The electricity is turned off in his cell so he cannot use his radio or TV.

Anyone who refuses a direct order and does not cuff up is inviting the goon squad to beat them. The officers enjoy these events because it gives an opportunity for the newer officers to be trained in the proper method of forcibly removing a prisoner from his cell. After a while, even the dumbest prisoners realize the futility of it all.

About four years ago, the prison decided to contract out the food services to a private vendor. The prison had been paying out $3 a day per prisoner for food. At first, with the change to the private vendor, it still did. The same six-week rotational menu was still used, but because the vendor must make a profit, the quality and quantity were severely diminished. It was to the advantage of the prison to contract out the food services. Salaried kitchen workers could be transferred to fill the high shortage of correctional officers. In addition, with lowered quality and quantity, food could be used as a punishment.

With the state budget cutbacks, a concerted effort has been undertaken to reduce the amount and quality of the food served in Arizona prisons. Understandably, this is a sensitive issue for prisoners. Food is the single-most basic thing in a prisoner's life. When they mess with our food it is cruel and unusual punishment. Bad food is the most common reason for prison riots.

New procedures have been phased in, which involve reducing the number of calories provided each day, paying more attention to the portion size, using less costly foods, and reducing the meals on Saturday, Sunday and holidays to two meals. In SMU II, the control unit we were moved to in 1997, hot lunches have been eliminated and a cold, sack lunch of low-quality luncheon meat and bread has been substituted. We no longer get fruit with lunch or dinner. Fruit juice has been eliminated and packets of powdered fruit drink mix, which are mostly sugar, have been substituted. Thus not only are there fewer calories, but the nutritional value of those remaining is drastically reduced.

This program has been going on in Arizona for two years now. Other states, such as Iowa, Minnesota, North Carolina,

Virginia and Texas, have jumped on the bandwagon with the same reduced food programs. Some advocates for prisoners have said that these cuts are causing health problems. A criminal justice expert commented on the food cuts by saying, "[Savings are] always incredibly marginal and shows a lack of political will to take on the larger issues, like releasing non-violent offenders in order to get real savings."

Food costs are a very small portion of the overall prison budget. Aside from new prison construction, 80 percent of the budget goes for salaries of officers and personnel. In Texas, the 2003 budget had a shortfall of $9.9 billion. It was ordered that they cut five percent, or $230 million. Six million of that cut came from reducing the food budget. A spokesman for the department stated, "We emphasize portion control. Where in the past each prisoner was given two biscuits, he now receives one. When a chicken patty was served with macaroni and cheese, we now cut the macaroni and cheese. We also substitute cheaper cuts of meat."

We must wonder where this will end. We are being fed diets of sugar-laden calories, high in starches and carbohydrates, empty of nutrition. This combined with the elimination of work programs, exercise and lockdown conditions that keep us in our cells 23 hours a day causes serious obesity. Rather than providing adequate protein, vegetables and fruit, we are being fed like cattle being fattened for the slaughter. If prisoners look heavy, it gives the impression that we are being fed properly, but that is not the case.

Exercise and showers

Three times a week we receive exercise and a shower. Each pod has an enclosed exercise area in the back of the pod. It is smaller than most dog runs, measuring about eight by seventeen feet with four concrete walls and an open roof covered with steel mesh. There is no equipment such as a weight machine or a basketball hoop, just a small rubber ball to bounce off the walls. The exercise turns begin right after breakfast. On alternating days, the men upstairs and the men downstairs go out one at a time for one hour for exercise. The door to the exercise area opens and the prisoner enters. The manual lock is secured, the prisoner backs up to the tray slot in the door and the officer removes the handcuffs. After about an hour the officer returns and the prisoner is cuffed up again and returned to his cell. When he is back in his cell, the next person is allowed out.

After coming back in from exercise we are put in the shower. After grabbing the shower items, we are once again cuffed-up. Every time we leave the cell we are strip searched and cuffed behind our back, even for the shower. We take off all of our clothes and hand them to the officer so he can search them. Then we bend over and spread our cheeks, turn around and show the soles of our feet, lift our arms, run our hands through our hair, open our mouth and lift our testicles. We are handed back our clothes, and we get dressed. The shower is five feet from my cell, but I am still strip searched and cuffed up. If we request a razor, it is a cheap, disposable one and it is duly noted that we were issued a razor. When we are to be returned to our cell at the end of the shower we must give up the razor before we can leave the shower area. If we do not, the goon squad will be called. Razors are high-security items.

The shower room is a nasty, musty smelling little closet measuring five by six feet. There are no windows. It has a light and a showerhead. When you push the button, the water runs for ten minutes then shuts off automatically. For the next five minutes the water will not run again. Sometimes the water is hot, sometimes it is cold. Complaining does no good. We take what we get. Once we are in the shower, we do not get out until the officer returns for us. This can be fifteen minutes or it can be an hour. It is rarely short. There is little ventilation and a musty odor always lingers. If you are claustrophobic, the shower is not the place for you.

Smells and noise

The first thing you notice when stepping inside any prison cell-block is the putrid odor. All cell blocks smell, but they do not come close to death row. We all die a little bit each day on the row, and the odor accumulates and builds to an unbelievable level. There are 60 men in this cluster and we cannot escape the stink of fear, anger, rancid sweat, blood, stale urine, wasted semen, feces and flatulence. Once a week we are given a filthy sour mop, a broom and a toilet brush. No scouring powder is allowed, only watered-down liquid soap. There is no disinfectant. We must learn to live with the stench. If we are away from our cell for a few hours, such as at visitation, as soon as we step back into the pod, the odors smack us right in the face.

There are all kinds of vermin to deal with—families of field mice, scorpions, two-inch sewer roaches, cockroaches, black widow spiders, crickets, water bugs, grasshoppers, flies, moths, gnats, ants, and lots of mosquitoes. They come in under the doors, through the bars and the vents, or wiggle up through the sink drain. They are most active at night, so you wake up with bugs in your bed and bites all over your body. We learn to look inside our shoes before sticking our feet into them. Scorpions crave the warmth and darkness of shoes. It is excruciatingly painful to be stung by a scorpion who resents your foot intruding into its space.

Prison noises are haunting. Steel doors slamming all day and night. Alarms sounding, two-way radios blasting and intercoms blaring. With 60 prisoners in a cluster, one hears as many as 60 different conversations going on at a time. Men call out to friends in different pods to check on their welfare. When we can never get out of our cell and confront another prisoner, physical fights cannot occur. Angry men cuss at each other for hours. We cannot settle a grudge, so the prisoners become "cell warriors." The constant roar becomes a living, breathing entity of its own. It is not hard to go crazy from the din. It invades and pollutes our minds. We become desensitized to everything around us. We decay and rot like unpicked fruit.

Cells and property

Our cells are a spartan affair. A concrete tomb measuring seven by eleven feet. The walls, floor and ceiling have not been painted in years. There are no bars at the front of the cell like you see in the movies. The cell fronts are solid steel plate with thousands of half inch round holes. They allow for airflow and an unobstructed view of the prisoner. The front of the cell is about five feet wide, with a two foot offset enclosing the toilet and plumbing. The cell door is 30 inches wide and slides open electronically.

The bunk is a steel shelf that runs across the back wall and is seven feet from one side of the cell to the other. The bunk is 30 inches wide and 18 inches off the floor. The mattress is a sheet of foam rubber made in the prison industry yard. It is six feet long, thirty inches wide and is about three inches thick. It is encased in a heavy vinyl covering. The mattresses break down quickly and are seldom exchanged. A small metal shelf is welded to one of the sidewalls and serves as a table. It is 18 inches square and stands 30 inches off of the floor. It is better than nothing. The only seat is a 12 inches round disc 18 inches high, welded to the floor. The sink is a combination basin and commode made of stainless steel. The lower portion has the toilet bowl that is angled toward the front of the cell. At the top is a small basin without a stopper. A small spigot allows a quarter-inch stream of water to flow out about an inch high. When the water pressure is low, water just dribbles too slowly to drink. When the cold water button is pressed the water flows for one minute. The hot water runs for two minutes. After the water runs, it will not run again for five minutes. The same goes for the toilet. The toilet is of the modern water-saving design, and flushes with just one gallon. However, since the water pressure is often below normal, when it flushes the waste backs up into the bowl, where it will not flush again for five minutes. When the water pressure is low, it usually does not go back up to normal for an hour.

The light fixture is above the sink at the front of the cell. It is mounted above a sheet of polished chrome that is your mirror. The light fixture is 12 inches wide and has three fluorescent bulbs in it. Two are aimed downward providing the majority of the light. The bulbs are 36 watts. The third one is angled at the ceiling as a night light. It is on 24 hours a day, unlike the other lights which are turned off at 10 p.m. and go back on at 4.30

a.m. The night light is 7.5 watts, not bright enough to read by. It is just bright enough to allow the officers to see into the cell. The constant light causes sleep deprivation. It is part of the endless process of conditioning and breaking down the individual.

We are allowed three small cardboard boxes to hold our legal papers. All additional legal boxes must be put into storage. If we need to retrieve something from a stored box, we must contact the property officer, request that box and give up one of the boxes in our cell. The stated reason for this rule is that the boxes are a fire hazard because prisoners might be careless with cigarettes. In this control unit no smoking is allowed, but the rule remains the same. One box is supplied by the unit to store our personal property. Since we are allowed so little property, this is usually adequate. We are allowed to have a 13-inch TV and a small Walkman radio, and headphones must be used at all times. These items must be purchased by the prisoner from the prison store.

For some time I was fortunate enough to have a typewriter—a non-memory type, since memory typewriters are not permitted in prison. When they search our cells they want to be able to read everything possible. I had a typewriter because of an old rule. Non-memory typewriters are allowed in the rest of the prison, and I obtained mine when the death row prisoners were still housed there. In the death row control unit a typewriter is considered a weapon. Still, when we were moved to this unit, the few men who had non-memory typewriters were allowed to keep them for a while. A few months later, a new rule banned typewriters altogether.

SMU II has no windows. In our previous cellblock, at CB6, we had windows. We could see the outside world and breathe fresh air. We could smell the rain as it poured down. Once in a while we could see a star in the night sky. I had a ground-level cell and I could see the birds pecking around at the dirt for some morsel of food. The birds became my friends. I devised an ingenious method of throwing bits of bread out to them. I would roll up a sheet of paper into a straw-like tube then take old bread and wet it. I would then roll the dough into small pellets that fit into the tube. When the pellets dried, I could insert the tube through the half-inch holes of the window grill and shoot the bread out to my birds.

The birds learned to know when to come to my window. I used to feed them at 6:30 a.m., 12 p.m. and 6 p.m. I could set my watch by their chirping outside my window. The adult birds would eventually bring their baby chicks to feed. The babies could not eat on their own, so the adult birds would pick up the bits of bread and feed them from their beaks. They serenaded me with their chirping. One day as they were eating, I heard a frantic chirping coming from the birds that were sitting on the fence. A moment later I observed a large white cat on the prowl trying to sneak up on the birds. The cat was looking for a meal as well, but not bread. The birds were alarmed and flew away. When the cat left, they returned. I did not want to see any of my birds executed by that cat.

When we came to this prison and found that we had no windows, it was a terrible shock. Not having a window is one of the cruelest things that has been done to us. We have no portal to the outside world. We will never be able to see the night sky, or a star, or the moon again. A month after we were moved here, a bird was able to squeeze under the one-inch opening at the bottom of the exercise door. The bird flew around the entire pod for about an hour until the police chased it out. I like to think that the bird was looking for me.

SERVICES

Religious services

In all the other units we were allowed to attend religious services. At Central Unit there is an actual chapel. In CB6, we had services in the visitation room. In SMU II, for security reasons, no assembly of prisoners is permitted. There are no group activities.

A few volunteer chaplains of different faiths find their way around the cellblocks and stop in front of your cell and speak with you. They are not allowed to pass out any religious tracts. One does not need to be religious to want to see a chaplain. I have seen devout atheists ask to see a chaplain just to speak to a human being other than a prison guard. It is obvious to the chaplains when someone is not interested in religion, but the chaplains know that part of the religious experience is human contact so they don't mind obliging at times. I used to know a retired volunteer chaplain named George. He would come around and see me and occasionally go to see my folks. It felt like a support system, as if I was a part of a family. George eventually moved to another state. I love and miss him.

One must not confuse the compassion and understanding of a priest or minister in the free world with the service offered by the hired prison chaplain. His function is to go through the formalities of the system. He never comes around to the cellblocks to see the prisoners. When someone requests to be married, the prospective spouse must meet with the chaplain to convince the chaplain that the marriage is on the up and up. The prospective spouse is told what crime the prisoner committed just in case the prisoner never mentioned this. The chaplain must then sign a form approving the marriage.

The chaplain is supposed to console prisoners on the loss of a loved one. In December, 1996, an officer came to my cell and told me I was going to the counselor's office. I did not know why the counselor wanted to see me, but I went. When I reached his office, I could see through the window that the man inside was not the counselor. This man told me that he was the institutional chaplain and he had some bad news for me. He told me my father had passed away the day before. I asked him if he had any other details and he said no. Since I was allowed a bereavement phone call, he would permit me to phone my mother. He stayed in the room while I spoke to my mom. At the end of the call he tried to look sincere and asked if there was anything that he could do for me. I told him that I knew that the department of religion had greeting cards that were donated by card companies, and I asked him if he could give me a sympathy card to send to my mother. He asked me if I was indigent. I told him I was not. He said that he could not give me a card if I was not indigent. Trying to maintain my composure I explained to him that I had no problem paying for a sympathy card, but that it would take at least a week to get a card ordered through the commissary. I wanted to comfort my mom now. He said there was nothing he could do.

The institutional chaplain makes sure the death row prisoner has his religious needs attended to before his execution.

He usually sends someone to the cell to ask what the religious preference is and if there is a volunteer chaplain we wish to see prior to the execution. If we wish to have someone present at the execution to offer last rites, that will be arranged.

Medical treatment

When a prisoner needs medical treatment, he must fill out a form called a Health Needs Request (HNR). Emergencies are seen first, others in turn. When an officer comes to the cell to take us to sick call, we go through the entire strip-search routine. We are cuffed in front and a belly chain goes around our waist to allow some mobility while we are being examined. Sometimes they will place us in leg irons to walk to the medical unit.

A few years ago the prison started a policy of charging $3 per medical visit. The accompanying memo stated that this was being done to cut down on abuses of sick call and to have the prisoner give something back to the community for services received. Those who do not have any money in their prison accounts are not denied treatment, but liens are placed on their prison accounts, and whenever someone sends some money, the prison satisfies the arrears before crediting the prisoner with the balance.

There are certain chronic conditions that are seen every three months without charge. These are diabetes, cancer, hypertension, heart conditions, HIV and tuberculosis. All other chronic conditions are not covered.

Before getting to see a medical provider, we must first see a nurse on the "nurse's line." The nurse questions us about our problems, makes notations in the file and refers us to the "doctor's line." A few days to a week later we are taken to the doctor's line. We almost never see a medical doctor. We usually see an ANP (Adult Nurse Practitioner) who is a nurse certified to treat prisoners under the authority of a doctor's license. The ANPs can order medications and testing. Their requests for outside tests must be approved by a committee. For simple ailments, such as colds, flu and stomach aches, this system works, but serious conditions are frequently missed or incorrectly diagnosed. We can be taken to an outside hospital for testing and treatment only in the most serious situations, since death row prisoners are considered escape risks.

A number of prisons have begun using forms of HMOs (Health Maintenance Organizations) to handle their medical needs. Even in the free world, HMOs are notorious for keeping costs down and routinely ignoring requests for medical testing.

Filing a medical grievance rarely resolves anything. When a medical grievance is submitted, the FHA (Facility Health Administrator) reviews the complaint. I submitted an HNR for lower back pain. When I saw the nurse, I explained my problem. I requested that x-rays be taken. He told me he would pass me along to the medical provider. When nothing had happened after a week or two I made inquiries. I was told I did not have any back problems. In fact I have a 30 percent permanent disability in my back from a job-related accident. In a lot of pain and furious, I submitted a medical grievance. About a month later I received a response from the FHA: "You were seen on l/4/95 and you were given your high blood pressure medication and placed on a low fat diet. Nothing further is indicated." The date 1/4/95 was for a previous visit two years earlier. No one picked up on the error. The only thing one can do in such cases is to file a state or federal lawsuit, but this gets so involved that most prisoners do not go that far.

I have seen at least six men die of cancer or other major illnesses because they were not diagnosed early enough. Even when someone is dying of cancer, they are rarely given narcotic painkillers. One man died because the battery in his pacemaker gave out before it was replaced.

There is a medical epidemic that is rampant not only in Arizona but throughout the prison system in America—Hepatitis C Virus (HCV). In an article in the *Arizona Republic* newspaper, dated February 10, 2001, it stated "Of Arizona's 26,800 inmates in the prison system, an estimated 6,000 have Hepatitis C Virus. Of these, an estimated 700–1,000 meet the criteria making them eligible for treatment." Today there are over 31,000 prisoners in Arizona. In my prison unit, there is one person receiving treatment. The reason being is that it costs an average of over $8,000 to treat a prisoner per year. It would run into millions of dollars to begin treatment to tackle the problem. It is easier to turn a cold shoulder.

A case in point is a man diagnosed over 15 years ago with HCV. It was new then, and not much was known about treatment. He was told that it might never develop into a serious condition. That he might just be a carrier and never develop any of the symptoms. He was told there was no treatment. A few years ago Interferon was becoming standard treatment for HCV. The prison would not authorize it. Next, Ribavirin was developed and it was combined with the Interferon. He requested this treatment and was denied. Finally, a more effective Interferon called Pegylated Interferon combined with Ribavirin became the federal government approved treatment called Rebetron.

When he requested this treatment, he was told there was a new protocol. After a year of more blood tests he finally reached the point where he would have a liver biopsy. This took about a year to approve. At long last, he had the biopsy.

The biopsy confirmed his disease. He was told he has Stage 2 Chronic Active Hepatitis C with Fibrosis, which involved inflammation and early scaring (fibrosis) in one zone (portal) of the liver. The family nurse practitioner asked him if he wanted treatment or if he wanted to wait for a future treatment. He was told that the Rebetron treatment was only 15 to 25 percent effective. He told her that after 15 years of waiting, he would take the treatment now.

After an hour of signing release forms and waiting as the medial provider filled out the paperwork, she said there was a problem. Apparently, there is an enzyme called ALT, and a normal reading is 40. The department requires that at least double, 80, must appear in three blood tests over a two-year period. His last two tests were 82 and 78. She told him he could not be considered until he produces more tests of 80 or higher in the next year. She asked him how old he was. Almost 57, he told her. She said that once he reached 60, treatment is not authorized. He couldn't believe how depressed he felt.

He was beside himself and told me in confidence that now that he knows he has the terminal illness, and they continue to deny treatment, he feels as if he has been given a second death sentence. The big question is which one will kill him first: execution or liver failure?

The bill surely will come due. Since most prisoners are released back into society, they simply take the disease with them. It is transmitted through sex, blood transfusions or a minor fist-fight. It is wiser to treat it early rather than later when liver transplants are considered and the cost is ten times more expensive. HCV is a ticking time bomb for prisoners across the nation.

Dental care is terrible. The prison system is unable to attract qualified doctors, let alone dentists. Hardly any doctor or dentist with a practice on the outside would consider working in a prison, for economic reasons. The doctors in this prison are paid around $60,000 a year. Most doctors earn three times that on the outside. A number of prison doctors are hired when they have been seriously disciplined or even suspended from practicing medicine due to malpractice. The prison administration grants a special exception in these cases to fill its needs.

A dentist is rarely assigned full time to one particular unit. Usually he visits a unit once or twice a week. The dentist may see eight prisoners per day. Emergencies such as extractions and infections are seen first. Little regular treatment filters down to the majority of the waiting prisoners. Currently, it takes about a year to see a dentist for a filling. When your tooth gets so bad that you have severe pain, he will tell you that the tooth is beyond repair and he will pull it out. They would rather pull your teeth than save them. They can make you an inexpensive set of dentures and they are finished with you for good. You are charged $3 per visit. I have sometimes asked the dentist if he would do more than one procedure while I was in the office, since so much time is wasted in the transportation of the prisoner to the medical office. The answer is always no. You have received your issue of treatment and now you will have to wait again. So, you submit another HNR and wait another year.

Psychiatric services

With the closing of many mental hospitals in years past and the unprecedented construction of prisons in the last two decades, prisons have become the number one place to house the mentally ill. Jail populations have quadrupled in recent years. We have over 2 million people behind bars in America. It is estimated that a quarter of a million are mentally ill—12.5 percent. We have twice that percentage of men here on the row who are being treated with medication by the psychiatrist. At last count, there were 30 men out of the 115 on the row under treatment.

Life on death row was stressful enough at CB6, but when we were transferred to SMU II, stress and aggression soared through the roof. The standard operating procedure of the officers here is very confrontational. Attitudes and mannerisms seem designed to provoke conflict. The prison staff, the correctional officers, use a lot of psychology in the way they go about their daily business. Some methods are covert while others are overt. In this "pressure cooker" environment, most actions and reactions are deviously engineered by the staff for maximum effect. From years of experience they know all the buttons to push to get someone to go off. It is their game, their rules, and their prison.

I could not believe how freaked out I became as a result of the mistreatment I received when we first arrived. My level of anger was never higher. In the years I have been on death row, I have had a few bouts of anger and periods where I was upset at staff for one reason or another, but I had never before been at the point where I wanted to physically retaliate. I found myself fantasizing and dwelling on the thought of doing horrible and indecent things to certain officers if only the opportunity presented itself. I know that I was not alone. Just about every man in this pod has had the same feelings. I had to realize that I was functioning in a stimulus response syndrome. I had to keep telling myself that I would not allow myself to be pushed over the edge. The psychiatrist for death row is a forensic psychiatrist. He works part time for the prison. He comes in one day a week on a rotational basis. We first see the psychiatrist within two weeks of arrival, and he analyzes what we say are our problems. He starts us off on the medication he feels we need. When we go back, once a month, he sees how we are doing and adjusts the dosage, usually upward. The policy seems to be to over medicate. The staff feels safer if we are "out to lunch." The more we sleep, the better they like it.

After our level of medication is established, we go back to see the psychiatrist every month or so and he asks if we are doing okay. If we say we are okay, he says he will continue sending the medication and he will see us next time. That is it. There is no discussion of our problems. We do not lie on a couch. The drugs are our Band-Aid. There is no attempt to get to the root of the problem. When we see the psychiatrist there is no doctor/client confidentiality. Anything we tell him about our crime can be used against us in court.

Before my trial, I was warned by my attorney not to reveal anything to the psychiatrist. I did as I was told. As a result, the psychiatrist, when put on the stand, gave an incorrect evaluation of me. He stated that I showed no contrition for my crime. This negatively affected my sentencing. Two years later when I was back in the county jail to be resentenced, I accidentally ran into the psychiatrist. We spoke in his office and he saw another side of me. At the new hearing he testified that his original diagnosis of me was incorrect because I was instructed not to say much about myself prior to trial. He gave a very favorable report and stated that I certainly could be rehabilitated with a life sentence. But it was too little, too late. The judge was persuaded to impose the death sentence the first time around and would not change his mind.

In recent years, the number of issues that you can use to try to stop your execution have dwindled considerably. Since there are so many people on the row who suffer from mental problems, incompetency to be executed has become a major issue, with an incompetency defense raised in almost every case.

Legally, we cannot be executed if we do not know we are being punished. If we understand that we are to be executed for our deeds, then we are considered to be mentally competent. If we are incompetent and it is agreed that we are insane, the state will admit us to the mental hospital for treatment. The hospital staff is instructed to help return us to sanity. If and when that is accomplished, the state will transfer us back to death row to be executed. That policy has caused a dilemma in the medical community. The Hippocratic Oath instructs doctors to "do no harm." However, if a doctor contributes to returning a person to mental health only to be executed, then they are doing harm. A similar situation had arisen previously, when medical personnel were asked to prepare the condemned prisoners' arms for the intravenous line to feed the poison when the order is given for execution. Doctors do not participate in this practice. The prison must hire other personnel to do that. Doctors at the state mental hospital will no longer treat a prisoner who has been transferred from death row because he is deemed to be incompetent. But the state has not given up. It is now trying to get paramedics to do it.

PRISONER—ADMINISTRATION INTERACTION

The rules rule cleaning

After the move to SMU II, since we rarely leave our cells, the officers had to clean the pod area, to mop, sweep and dust the corridors. The officers really detested cleaning our pod, and this is probably why, although it took a year, the deputy warden decided that we were not the "mad dogs" they pictured us as being. A program was developed to allow one prisoner out of his cell without cuffs twice a day on a weekly rotational basis to clean the pod and his own cell. Here is a copy of the policy:

ARIZONA DEPARTMENT OF CORRECTIONS
ARIZONA PRISON COMPLEX—EYMAN
SPECIAL MANAGEMENT UNIT II
MEMORANDUM TO: Distribution
FROM: Dan Vannelli, Deputy Warden
DATE: July 6, 1998
SUBJECT: Death Row Portering

The following Death Row Portering procedure shall be implemented, effective immediately: All Death Row Inmates, with the exception of George cluster pod six (6) inmates and those inmates identified by the SMU II Administration will be given the opportunity to come out and clean their cells, pod, shower on their tier and recreation pens. The following will be strictly enforced and there will be no exceptions.

1. There will be two (2) inmates, one at a time, out per day per pod with the exception of Sunday to clean the above listed. This will be after the start of shift at approximately 1330 hours, and after the evening meal at approximately 1730 hours for about thirty (30) minutes.
2. The cells that are let out will be the first two recs for the day. The afternoon porter will be assigned to clean their cell, the top of the panel box, the railing, and the pod floor. The evening porter will be assigned to clean the shower the recreation pen and their cell.
3. All new death row inmates will not be allowed to come out of their cell for the first one hundred and twenty (120) days.
4. Any inmate, while portering, that tampers with a security device of any kind will be instructed to lock down, a disciplinary write up will be issued, and they will lose their porter privilege for the extent of their stay at SMU II. There will be no exceptions!
5. If an inmate is caught passing any item to another inmate, they will be instructed to lock down, an Incident Report (IR) written, and a disciplinary write up issued. Also, their porter privilege will be revoked for ninety (90) days.

6. Any inmate that is not working or doesn't meet the cleaning expectations of the designated shift supervisor, will lose their porter privileges for sixty (60) days.
7. If an inmate stops working and stands in front of another inmate's cell for any reason, the inmate will be instructed to lock down, an IR will be written, and a disciplinary write up issued. Also their porter privilege will be revoked for thirty (30) days.
8. All inmates must be properly dressed when leaving their cell. This includes deck shoes and jump suit that will be worn in the correct manner.
9. Inmates must follow the direction of the officers assigned. If not, they will be instructed to lock down, an IR will be written and a disciplinary write up issued. Also, their porter privilege will be revoked for thirty (30) days.
10. A courtesy shower will be allowed IF the inmate completes the assignment and the expectations for cleaning are met.
11. If an inmate loses his porter privilege three (3) times within the same year, he will not be allowed to porter for the extent of his stay at SMU II.
12. The assigned CO III will keep a record of the inmates not ever allowed to porter and those that have lost their porter privilege for whatever offense. The list will be updated weekly and it will include when the inmates get their privilege back. This list will be given to the swing shift commander on each Friday by the end of the CO III's shift.
13. See attached list of inmates restricted from participation.

That method of allowing the prisoners to do their own cleaning lasted about six months. They finally determined that it was too much of a security risk to allow us out of our cells for that so the program was ended. Then, for a long time the pods were uncared for. Reluctantly, the officers returned to sweeping and mopping the pods once a week. But the officers resented being required to perform menial, porter's cleaning chores in front of prisoners. So, finally, the warden decided to allow a cleaning crew of prisoners from a different unit, other than death row, to come in and clean.

Commissary

There is a prison commissary from which we can order various items weekly. In past years there were food items on the store list that enabled us to cook a meal in the small hot pots we were allowed to have as the result of a court-ordered consent decree in 1973. We were allowed to receive three 25-pound food packages each at Christmas and the hot pots were included. With the food as bad as it is, being able to heat up some soup or some chili con carne was a salvation. But the prison decided the hot pots were a threat to security. A prisoner who was upset might heat up some water and toss it on an officer. The prison tried to eliminate the hot pots, but they were always unsuccessful. So they used a different method. They removed from the commissary store list just about everything that could be cooked in a hot pot. About the only thing left on the list to use in the hot pots was instant coffee. Finally in 1997 the prison succeeded in getting the consent decree modified to eliminate the Christmas food packages and the hot pots. A 25-year era was over.

The current store list has virtually no food items worth buying. The only things on it are basic hygiene items and junk food like candy bars, cookies and chips. There are still a few selected food items and instant coffee to supplement the standard meals.

In the past, the profits from the commissary flowed into the prison Arts and Recreation Fund. This money was used to purchase exercise and recreational items for the prisoners and to repair broken equipment. The fund also paid for the upkeep of the law library. But then all the weight machines and loose weights were removed, and the law libraries were closed. So the prison got the state legislature to change the law to allow it to use the Arts and Recreation Fund to pay for any piece of state property that was broken or destroyed by a prisoner. It also permitted the funds to be used to pay the medical bills of prisoners and officers involved in any fights. The fund has thus been gutted and no money remains for any prisoner benefit whatsoever.

Law libraries

In a continuing effort to eliminate more and more prisoners' rights, the prison had been restricting certain areas of access to the courts. In 1990 a prisoner named Fletcher Casey and 22 other inmates filed a class action lawsuit in the federal district court in Phoenix. One of their claims was that they were being denied effective access to the courts. The ACLU National Prison Project took up the case on behalf of the inmates. The case was heard by federal judge Carl Muecke who ruled in favor of the inmates and issued an injunction that set forth detailed and system-wide changes for all Arizona prison law libraries and the legal assistance programs.

The ruling mandated the number of hours for prison courses, the qualifications required for the instructor (an outside-certified paralegal, trained law student or attorney), class content (one third of the time to be spent on lectures, two thirds on fundamentals of research and writing), and the method of testing (written exam, pass/fail).

The department told the media and public that this was costing the taxpayers untold dollars. In fact all the program consisted of was a multi-hour videotape that was played for less than a dozen inmates every six months or so.

Also included in the Casey v. Lewis lawsuit was a list of law books to be maintained in the libraries. Most of the 34 existing law libraries already had those volumes. However, the Department of Corrections convinced the general public that the cost of the law libraries was coming out of the taxpayers' pocket. The authorities never told the public that the libraries were paid for by the inmates' own Arts and Recreation Fund.

The state did not like the outcome of the lawsuit, so it appealed the decision to the Ninth Circuit Court of Appeals. The Ninth Circuit rejected the claim and upheld the decision of the lower court. With the conservatives in the majority in most of the country, and riding the wave of mean spiritedness toward prisoners in general, the state decided to appeal the Ninth Circuit decision to the US Supreme Court on a writ of certiorari. This is not an automatic appeal. You must brief the court and ask if they will accept your case. The party bringing such requests is unsuccessful 97 percent of the time. It is only special cases that are taken on by the court. However, since Chief Justice Rehnquist and Justice O'Connor are both conservatives and both from the state of Arizona, it came as no surprise that the court accepted the case.

When the decision was announced, Justice Scalia, writing for the majority, said that inmates could not be guaranteed the wherewithal to transform themselves into litigation engines capable of filing everything from shareholder derivative actions to slip-and-fall claims. The tools required to be provided are those that the inmates need in order to attack their sentences, directly or collaterally, and in order to challenge the conditions of their confinement. Impairment of any other litigation capacity was simply one of the incidental (and perfectly constitutional) consequences of conviction and incarceration. The Supreme Court also said that Judge Muecke's order was "inordinately, indeed wildly intrusive."

After this decision, the Department of Corrections in Arizona closed all the law libraries. All of the books were given away. A paralegal has been hired to supply legal forms pertaining to Habeas Corpus Petitions, Civil Rights (1983) Federal lawsuits, and Post Conviction Relief. The prisoner has to pay for the forms, and the paralegal cannot assist him in the lawsuit. He or she can only show the prisoner how to fill in the blanks. The director stated on TV that once the inmate has filed the forms in the court, the court will appoint an attorney to assist the inmate. That is not so. I have personally handled five Civil Rights complaints for inmates and not once were we granted an attorney to assist us. Without access to law books to obtain case law and citations that relate to the case, it is almost impossible to prevail.

Visitation

The prison describes the purpose of visitation as: "to … permit family members to visit inmates for the purpose of maintaining both family and community ties." That gives the impression that prison officials think visitation is important and that they encourage it. That is not exactly true.

Since visitation is considered a "privilege," the prison authorities have the right to approve or deny whoever they choose. There is a mass of rules and regulations aimed at restricting, denying and suspending visits. There are rules for strip searching of visitors and searching their vehicles. Visitors are treated as if they were prisoners themselves.

There have been many changes in the visitation procedures for death row. At CB6 there was a condemned row program that allowed individuals who maintained excellent behavior to win certain privileges. One of these privileges was full and limited contact visits rather than the normal visitation through a glass partition. It took years of perfect behavior and no disciplinary write-ups to qualify, but if you could have a contact visit with a loved one it was worth whatever you had to go through. We lost all of this when we were moved to this control unit. The visitation procedure here at SMU II is as follows.

Each prisoner can have ten people on his visitation "Ten List." To place someone on a visitation list, you request an application be sent to the individual who wants to visit. That person fills it out, mails it back to the prison visitation office where it is processed. The prison runs the application through the NCIC (National Crime Information Computer) and the

ACIC (Arizona Crime Information Computer) to see if there are any convictions or outstanding warrants. Even a misdemeanor can disqualify a visitor. A denial can be appealed to the complex warden within ten days. His decision is final.

When a visitor is approved his or her phone number is verified, listed in the files and placed on the computer that permits phone calls. A prisoner can only phone the ten people on their visitation list. If they have no visitors, they can make no phone calls. Phone calls are collect and last for ten minutes, every eight days.

In-state visitors can come once a week for two hours after phoning for an appointment. These are non-contact visits through a glass window with no phone, and you have to yell to be heard over all the other visitors in the same room. Out of state or foreign visitors can come only after submitting a special visitation application and having it approved. Then they can come over a three-day weekend.

The Arizona Department of Corrections does not allow members of the press or media to conduct face-to-face interviews with prisoners. Interviews are permitted only by phone or letter. Phone calls are monitored and recorded, mail is opened, inspected and read.

Most prisons are located in rural areas which are difficult for the visitor to reach. Out of state and foreign visitors have great difficulty finding the prison.

There is a strict dress code for visitors: no sheer, see-through or open-netted clothing, no bare midriff or strapless tops, no tube tops, halter tops or body suits, no shorts or skirts shorter than mid-thigh when seated. Clothing tops must be cut no lower than the collarbone in front and back.

Underwear and shoes must be worn. Denim, including jeans, or international orange colored garments are strictly forbidden.

At CB6, prisoners wore blue denim. Then the no-denim rule made sense, so that visitors would not be mistaken for prisoners trying to escape. But, in this control unit we now wear bright orange jump suits. Nonetheless the old, no-denim rule, is still enforced.

One Sunday morning, I was locked in the visitation room cage, waiting for my friend Jack to visit. All the other visitors came in, but no Jack. After a while, one of the officers came to tell me that Jack would be a few minutes late. She did not say why. Finally, Jack entered. As he walked around the visitation desk, which was in the center of the room, I could see that he was wearing a large, plaid-design Scottish kilt or dress!

Every visitor and every prisoner in the room turned to stare at Jack. No sound could be heard. After this surreal moment passed, I asked Jack what was going on. He explained that since prisoners were now wearing the orange jump suits, he assumed that he could wear blue jeans. But the visitation officers refused to allow him to enter wearing blue jeans. A supervisor was summoned. The supervisor confirmed the ban on blue jeans. Jack thought a minute. He asked whether there was any rule against wearing a dress. The supervisor considered this carefully. Finally he answered that, no, there was no rule against a dress. Jack went back to his car. In the trunk he had a large, plaid tablecloth he used for picnics. He wrapped that around his waist and cut a hole for the belt to hold the dress up.

After all the visitors left, I was inundated with questions from all the other prisoners. Weeks later at visitation, I was still being asked about it.

Attorneys visit during the week. These are also non-contact visits. The prisoner is locked in a small room with a large glass window and there are windows in the solid doors behind the attorney's side and behind the prisoner so the police can observe what is going on. To pass documents back and forth there is a slot in the wall with room for just one sheet of paper at a time. Years ago we were allowed full contact visits with our attorneys, but this is now seen as a security threat. Even though the prisoner is strip searched before and after the visit, the prison authorities are uncomfortable with any physical contact.

When a prisoner finishes a legal visit, he is not immediately returned to his cell. Instead, he is escorted to the property room where he is placed in a five by five feet holding cell and required to get naked for a body search. After that search, he is seated in a magnetometer chair. It is a large black chair that looks like the outmoded electric chair. The chair functions as a metal detector. If one has any metal implanted in their body the bells and whistles go off. They want to determine whether the prisoner has swallowed any metal or secreted any metal in their body cavities. This is in spite of the fact that the attorney cannot pass anything except paper through the paper slot provided.

Inmate grievance system

Stated policy (from the Arizona Department of Corrections "Stated policy"): The department's inmate grievance process provides inmates with timely, fair and decisive remedies to complaints that might otherwise unnecessarily burden the courts.

In fact every possible way to deny a grievance is used. Grievances can be denied even before being logged in as a formal grievance. The average prisoner without much education or patience will file a grievance in good faith only to have it returned unprocessed due to some procedural fault, such as not starting off with the proper opening statement or exceeding the ten day filing limit.

Each prison unit has an assigned grievance coordinator who provides grievance forms, and logs in and assigns case numbers to each grievance. There are specific steps and time frames involved in filing and processing a grievance.

The first step is to file what is called an informal grievance resolution with an assigned counselor. He investigates your complaint and either finds your complaint correct or denies it. If it is denied, the prisoner has ten days to file a formal grievance with the coordinator. If the prisoner does not attempt to informally resolve his complaint, the formal grievance will not be processed and will be automatically denied. The maximum length of time for completion of a grievance is 90 days. Expiration of the time limit at any level will prevent it from proceeding to the next level unless there is an agreement in writing to an extension of time.

The grievance coordinator has 30 days to answer a formal grievance. If it is denied (almost always), there are ten days to file an appeal of the denial with the unit warden or deputy warden. Within 20 days one receives a response. If denied, there are ten days to appeal the warden's decision to the director's office in Phoenix. The answer is supposed to come in 20 days but it rarely does. That is the last appeal and that decision is final. Then we are entitled to proceed to state or federal court.

The disciplinary system

> Stated policy: The department uses a formal disciplinary system to impose penalties on inmates who violate the department's policies, procedures or regulations.

Although there has always been a disciplinary system, the current one ensures conviction and total lack of fairness.

Prior to the Lewis v. Casey lawsuit that closed the law libraries and effectively ended legal representatives, the prisoner had a chance to win at a hearing. There was an actual hearing at which we could have a street attorney come and plead the case before the committee. If someone could not afford an attorney, he could have a prisoner legal assistant represent him at the hearing. In the disciplinary courtroom there was the coordinator who prosecuted the charge, the disciplinary chairman, one uniformed officer and a non-security person such as a secretary. Both sides could call witnesses. We could cross-examine the witnesses. At the end, both sides would make a summation. Both sides would leave the room and the three officers would decide the case. We would be called back in and the decision and penalty would be announced. Only major violations were handled at the disciplinary hearings. Minor violations were always handled outside the hearing by the disciplinary coordinator. If some doubt existed at the hearing, the committee could just reduce the charge to a minor violation. In this way your prison custody level would not rise, although the loss of privileges would be the same as if it were a major violation. Although far from perfect, this system gave us a chance to prove our innocence and to participate. The current system does not. We have no right to counsel or to question witnesses. It is all in the hands of the disciplinary hearing officer.

Shortly after we were moved to this control unit, I made a drawing of my cell and pod area to satisfy the curiosity of my pen pals. I sent the drawing out to a dear friend who made copies and returned them to me. When the copies arrived at the prison mailroom, they were seized and turned over to the investigation personnel. I was called out of my cell and confronted with the copies. I was asked what they were for. I told the truth, that they were simply cell drawings to show curious friends what a cell looked like in a control unit. This explanation was not accepted. They told me my drawing was an "escape plan."

I tried to argue. "If this is an escape plan, why did I have copies sent into the prison instead of trying to sneak them out?" I pointed out that my drawing showed no hallways or doors, no views of the building, inside or out, no roads or highways to be used in a getaway. I added that I had made a drawing of every cell I had ever been in. "Nobody ever complained before."

At the disciplinary hearing, the Designated Hearing Officer (DHO) read the charges and showed me the evidence. I could not believe my eyes. Instead of the drawing I made of the control unit cell, he had a cell drawing from CB6 which had been used as an exhibit in a federal court hearing.

I pushed the copy back to the DHO, pointed to the identification "Cell drawing CB6" typed in the lower left-hand corner, and explained about the previous lawsuit. He acknowledged that the drawing did not represent a cell in SMU II. I then added that if a document is used in a court proceeding, as this drawing was, it becomes a matter of court record and cannot be considered contraband. After listening to me, he announced: "You are guilty." I protested. He looked me in the eye and declared: "It is my duty to find you guilty!"

You can appeal such a decision to the coordinator of discipline and then to the unit warden. They will both read the case and ensure that there was "some evidence" used to convict you to uphold the findings. You can then appeal to the Hearing Officer at the Central Office. Regretfully, this is a rubber stamp of the unit decision. (See Appendix, p228, for a list of the disciplinary charges and penalties.)

The mail system

> Stated policy: The Department has an established system of mail and property for inmates. The Department order establishes allowable property limits and methods of accountability, and provides for disposal of unclaimed property and contraband. Inmates are encouraged to correspond through the mail with whom they choose, subject to the limitation outlined in the order.

Mail is a major concern for both the prisoners and the prison. There is tight control of both incoming and outgoing mail. A prisoner lives for mail. It is the most important link between the prisoner and the outside world. I have known men to order seed catalogs just to have some mail arrive when they do not have letters coming from friends and family.

Every night at the end of the day shift's tour an officer pushes your mail through the half-inch space under your cell door. When we receive mail it is already open and stamped "inspected" on the envelope. The policy states that all incoming mail shall be read or censored. If one is under investigation for anything, they will read 100 percent of the mail and make copies of anything they consider relevant before sending it on. Seized materials from incoming letters and packages are returned to the sender or held for 90 days. The prisoner pays the postage for outgoing seized property. After 90 days, items not returned are destroyed.

We are not permitted to receive letters from ex-inmates who are under supervision by the department, or another prisoner in any correctional institution, except for immediate family. We cannot write to victims of the crime or their families unless approved by the warden. If anyone advises the warden that they do not wish to receive mail from us, we are forbidden to write to that person. We cannot write to another with the intent to plot, scheme or conspire to defraud, or in anyway illegally solicit assistance. No sweepstakes or contest material are authorized. We cannot indulge in lotteries or games of chance.

Incoming legal mail is logged on a sheet and delivered to the inmate, opened in their presence and checked for contraband. Official policy is that this type of mail will not be read or censored. In practice, it happens. At CB6 my legal mail was opened six times outside of my presence, and in the years here at SMU II it has occurred several times. We find the legal mail mistakes when we receive our regular mail, and we come across a letter from our attorney that has been opened and stamped "inspected." When we file a grievance of the violation of our legal mail rights, we are told that due to the large volume of incoming mail, once in a while a letter from an attorney will not be detected until after it goes through the automatic letter opener. You are assured that it was a mistake and that your mail was not read. They promise you it will not happen again. But it does.

At night we push our outgoing mail under our door for the graveyard shift officers to pick up. Usually our mail reaches the post office the next day, but policy permits the prison to hold our mail up to 36 hours before delivery to the post office. The prison has the right to read all outgoing correspondence, except for family mail. Family mail cannot be censored or read, but can be inspected for contraband. We are never told what constitutes contraband. That policy leaves the door open for all of our outgoing mail to be opened and inspected.

Just recently, the rules on outgoing legal mail were changed. We are not allowed to seal the envelope of our outgoing legal mail. An officer will come by to pick it up and he will open the envelope to inspect the contents for contraband. Then he will seal the envelope and stamp it as having been "inspected." He is then supposed to list the envelope on the legal mail log sheet. I have often asked what kind of contraband are they looking for. No one seems to know, although there is a story about someone mailing feces out as legal mail. Recently I was told by an officer inspecting my outgoing legal mail that he is checking for money and drugs. My reply to that was, "That's crazy, prisoners do not send drugs out in the mail, they try to smuggle drugs in through the mail!"

An indigent person is allowed to send out three one-ounce pieces of first class mail per week free. Recent new rules forbid friends and family from sending stamps in their letters to a prisoner. The only way we can obtain stamps now is to purchase them from the prison. The prison recommends that friends and family send money orders to the prisoner to permit stamp purchases from the commissary. Over the years I have been on the row, I have observed that people will gladly send an occasional book of stamps in a letter, but if we have to ask for a money order it complicates the relationship. People do not care to send money. They will send magazine subscriptions and books but not money.

No reason was given for this policy change. The prison only sells the current one-ounce, 37-cent, first class postage stamps. The post office requires 23 cents more for each additional ounce. If we can only buy 37-cent stamps, then we waste money by adding a second 37-cent stamp to our letter instead of a 23-cent stamp, simply because we cannot buy them. In my particular case, most of my mail goes to Europe. A one-ounce letter costs 80 cents. I have to use three 37-cent stamps and waste 31 cents because they will not sell 80-cent stamps.

Recently the number of stamps that we can purchase from the commissary has been reduced from 40 per week to 20. The number of envelopes we can purchase has been reduced from 50 to 20. No reason was given for this change. I submitted a grievance on this issue. I was simply told that the limit of stamps and envelopes allowed for purchase per week was 20 each. Still no reason given.

There are also rules and regulations concerning the censorship of books, magazines and other publications. They must all come directly from the publisher or a store. If any items are determined to represent a threat to security, the warden may restrict these publications. The decision of the warden is final.

Telephone calls

Phone calls are even more closely monitored than mail. The person you wish to call must be one of the people on your visitation "Ten List." Once the person is approved to visit, they must phone the visitation office to have their phone number verified. They are told to hang up and the visitation officer calls them back immediately. The prisoner then submits a form to have the phone number added to his/her phone list in the computer.

If a prisoner is on restriction because of a disciplinary write-up, he is not permitted to make a phone call. Phone calls are a privilege, not a right. The phone calls are collect and are for ten minutes only. A little-known fact is that prison phone calls are a major source of income for the prison and state. The prison takes bids for the yearly contracts from the major phone companies to install and maintain the phone equipment. In Arizona and most other states, a large kickback or commission is paid for the service contract. The Department of Corrections in Arizona receives approximately $1.5 million a year from their service provider as well as receiving a percentage of the overall yearly billing amount.

The reason so much money is involved is because neither the prisoner nor the party he calls has any choice about the rate charged per minute. The long-distance collect rate is 20 times a regular rate. A lot of money is made on the backs of the usually poor family members who have no other choice but to pay the outrageous phone rates if they wish to speak to their loved ones. Currently there is a $3 surcharge and a $1 per minute rate for these calls. A ten-minute phone call costs $13 plus tax.

When the prisoner wants to make a collect phone call, he must turn in a phone call request slip the night before his weekly phone day. We must fill in our name, the name and number of the person we wish to call, the person's relationship to us, and the date of the call. The next night an officer will come to our cell and put us into handcuffs that are attached to a belly chain. We are escorted to the phone that is mounted on the wall at the front of the pod. Our cuffed, chained hands can just barely reach the receiver and the keypad. We must learn how to nuzzle the receiver on our neck as we attempt to push the buttons on the phone. Once we dial a number, a recording comes on and asks us to speak our name, which is then recorded. If the number rings through, the party answering will hear our recorded voice saying our name and the caller is instructed to press a number to accept the call or to hang up to refuse it. We can then have a ten-minute conversation that is interrupted every minute with another recorded message that states: "This call is from an inmate." A warning is given when two minutes are left and when 30 seconds are left. The calls are automatically disconnected at the end of the ten-minute period.

Since it is such an inconvenience for the guards to come and get us and hook us up to the belly chain and take us out of our cell, once we are at the phone we get only one attempt to reach our party. If we get a busy signal, no answer, or a busy circuit signal, we cannot try again until the next week.

TV watching

In the concerted effort by the Department of Corrections to take away just about every item of personal property authorized in years past, the one major item that has survived is the TV. By allowing the prisoners to have TV, the prison creates a built in baby-sitting device. When the prisoners are busy watching TV, they are not planning mischief or evil deeds against the prison. It is to the benefit of the prison to make TV addicts out of the entire prisoner population. This is one area of penal psychology the prisoners readily submit to.

TV watching becomes a sociological phenomenon. If we hear it once, we hear it 50 times a day: "What are you watching?" From 6 a.m. to midnight the TVs are on. Within the ten-man pod, factions develop. Small groups of two to four prisoners form TV-watching alliances. Most of them watch situation comedies, but some watch dramas or nature shows. Others watch cartoons. After dinner, we can hear these groups talking about which shows they plan to watch that evening. It is not uncommon for people to get upset at others if they choose not to watch a particular program on a particular night. Things get so regimented that normal conversation is delayed until the commercials come on. Events are planned around the commercial breaks. Some of the conversation you overhear can be easily confused—discussions of who died, who is cheating on another, who is a liar and so on. It took me some time to realize that this banter came from watching the daily soap operas.

When a new movie comes on the TV most of the pod is going to watch it, it is the closest thing to a group activity a man on death row can experience. It is like going to a theatre. When the entire pod watches a movie together (each man in his own isolated cell), it is as good as it gets. Guys call out and make remarks, laugh and joke. It is an interaction rarely seen on the row.

THINGS CHANGE DAILY

When one prisoner does something wrong, we are usually all made to suffer the consequences. We lose property items or privileges. When a few prisoners in the complex committed suicide by using their shoelaces to hang themselves, the goon squad came around and took not only the shoelaces, but the shoes as well. When someone was found to be concealing something inside of a bar of soap, they took all of the soap bars. Now we can only purchase those tiny little bars of soap you find in motel rooms. When someone tried to stick an officer with a pencil, they took all the pens and pencils. Now we can only buy the pen refills, we cannot have the plastic pen barrels. The only pencils we can have are the miniature three-inch ones like those used at the golf course. The other day they went through all of our legal papers and documents looking for staples. Someone had made a blow dart, affixed a staple to the end, and blew the dart at an officer. We are told that if we are now found with a staple, we will be given a major disciplinary write up for possession of a weapon! Now all staples are removed from incoming magazines. When someone squirted an officer with some liquid from an empty 16-ounce shampoo bottle, they took all the large shampoo bottles and now we can only buy four-ounce bottles of shampoo. The quality brands of shampoo do not come in four-ounce bottles.

The latest event occurred just the other day. Pod six houses the ten most disruptive prisoners on death row. One of those men was outside in the exercise area and refused to cuff up and come back into the pod. He was given a direct order to cuff up. He refused. The officer in charge thought he might have a shank (homemade knife). He called the goon squad. Dozens of police arrived in full battle gear with the German shepherd attack dog. When the prisoner still would not cuff up, the order was given to gas him. Mace or an Israeli Fogger was used.

When gas is sprayed anywhere in the cluster, it eventually circulates to everyone through the ventilation system. Since pod six is right next-door to my pod, we always get it the worst. I woke up gasping and coughing. The best way to minimize the effects of the gas is to wet a towel and throw it over your head. It does not eliminate the gas, but it helps. For an hour afterwards we continued to suffer.

CHAPTER 3

POLITICS OF DEATH AND THE DEATH ROW CHAIN GANG

The Georgia death penalty was declared unconstitutionally vague because jurors could not mete out the death penalty without standards to guide their decisions. All the states that had a death penalty, including Arizona, applied it in the same manner. And all had their death penalty statutes invalidated.

Those convicts on death row in Arizona at that time were resentenced to life. Each state was required to rewrite its death penalty statutes and have the new statutes approved by the US Supreme Court before it could start sentencing convicts to death again. From 1972 to 1976 there were no executions in the United States. By 1976, death sentences were declared constitutional again. The first execution to take place after the moratorium was of Gary Gilmore, who chose the firing squad. Utah still had the firing squad as a legal method of execution. Gilmore was executed on January 17, 1977.

In 1978, the Arizona Supreme Court declared Arizona's rewritten death penalty statute unconstitutional because it limited the evidence defendants could present on their behalf at the sentencing hearing. The statutes were revised to include this factor. The Ninth Circuit Court of Appeals certified the new law as constitutional in 1982. This caused the judges to give new sentences to each Arizona death row prisoner. All of those people who were on death row were resentenced. Most, if not all, of them were resentenced to death again. Six years later the Ninth Circuit Court of Appeals found the same statute unconstitutional in the sentence given to death row prisoner Jeffrey Allen Walton. The basis for that decision was that, like all those condemned to death in Arizona, the judge was the one who assessed the death sentence instead of a jury. On appeal, the US Supreme Court overturned the Ninth Circuit Court's decision and ruled in June 1990 that Arizona's death penalty law was constitutional. Finally, the state was able to resume executing its citizens. With the 29-year hiatus in Arizona—the last execution was in 1963—politicians were not very happy at the lack of executions. The conservative politicians called for speeding up the executions and cutting the gains the prisoners had made over the years. The major catchphrase they used was that the federal judges were engaging in "judicial activism" and were micromanaging the state prisons and blocking executions with endless stays of execution. Arizona's Republican governor Fife Symington was up for reelection in 1994. He was also under scrutiny for a program he instituted called "Project Slim" in which he claimed to be cutting administrative waste. It was becoming a scandal. He needed to find a way to distract public attention from this matter. He accomplished that by decrying the intrusion of the federal courts into the state prisons and especially by calling for quicker executions. Execution warrants were issued at an incredible rate, even though most of them were premature. This was done just to remind the condemned that the state was eagerly waiting to execute them.

I received one of these premature execution warrants on June 30, 1996—a copy of it is in the Appendix. It had been filed on June 25 and set the date of my execution for July 24. There was no way I should have received this warrant at this time. I was just in the door of the Federal District Court, so I had my entire habeas corpus petition yet to be processed before I would have to start worrying about a death warrant. Although I knew this was an error, I wondered if it was not a result of the state wanting to stick it to me for all the anti-prison articles I had written. I did some very heavy worrying. I was being forced to consider the fact that I was going to be killed by the state, and it did not feel good.

I asked my attorney why this warrant was issued in the first place. She spoke to the death penalty clerk at the federal court, who was as surprised to hear about the warrant as we were. The only reason she came away with was that it was the state's way of putting pressure on me, of telling me that they want me to know they intend to kill me. Indeed, before I received a stay, I got all kinds of signs from the administration that plans were being readied for my demise. I was served with all the appropriate forms to be filled out—such things as my last meal, who will attend hearings, disposition of my property, etc (again, these are reproduced in the appendices). I had deadlines for each form. I was going to be moved Tuesday, 9th July to an observation cell for the remaining two weeks until 48 hours before the actual time. Then I would be transported to the death house. It has never been the thought of death that has bothered me. At the proper time, when I know all my avenues of appeal are finished, I will have said my goodbyes and have everything in order. However, when this warrant came down unexpectedly I was taken off balance. I was simply not ready. The thought of my life ending in 30 days was startling. How does one cram 49 years of life into 30 days?

The chain gang

In the same time period, in 1992, the voters of Maricopa County, Arizona elected a new sheriff, Joe Arpaio. He declared himself "the toughest sheriff in America." He took away just about everything a prisoner in the county jail once was allowed to have both in personal property as well as food. He bragged about how he feeds his prisoners for 30 cents per meal. He feeds them green bologna and charges the prisoners a dollar a day for food. He recently went on TV to brag about the fact that he spends more money ($1.10) per day to feed his police dogs. He not only took away the *Playboy* magazines but even the coffee. No one gets a cup of coffee in Joe Arpaio's jail.

When the state of Alabama reintroduced the chain gang to put the prisoners to work, Arpaio jumped on the bandwagon and announced that he too would put his prisoners to work on a chain gang. He had already required that everyone wear pink underwear. This was because he had noticed that lots of pairs of underwear were disappearing. He claimed that the prisoners being released were stealing the underwear. As it later turned out, his own officers were found to be stealing the underwear. To make the underwear undesirable to steal, he had it all dyed pink. He brought back white uniforms with black horizontal stripes like the kind worn by prisoners of old. He put prisoners with disciplinary problems to work on road maintenance, cleaning and digging graves in the paupers' cemetery. He had become the "meanest sheriff in the nation," and was very proud of it. He put the overflow prisoners into army surplus tents in an annex. He wrote a book and went on TV and talk shows. A local newspaper called him "Joke Arpaio." Nonetheless, the citizens of Maricopa County re-elected him in 1996, and again in 2000.

Arizona's Governor Symington seized upon the popularity of using a chain gang and decided to adopt it, too. The Arizona Department of Corrections Director, Sam Lewis, started to use general population prisoners on work details on the prison grounds and along the highways. No chains were used, but it was a work detail none the less. Death row was not included in this chain gang.

Besides the "Project Slim" problem, Governor Symington had other legal troubles. He was under investigation by the federal government concerning allegations of fraud regarding some failed real estate projects that went into bankruptcy. There were 23 grand jury indictments against him. Most of the counts were for fraud, but one was for threatening a major credit union that he owed money to—if they did not give him some favorable terms and delays, he would have a state agency that was a tenant in one of the projects move out of the building and cause a major financial catastrophe to the project. This was a major offense, extortion, and grounds to remove him from office. In the end, Symington was found guilty of seven felony fraud counts and was removed from office. President Clinton, before leaving office, granted Symington a pardon.

But at that time, in 1995, Symington created another diversion by announcing a program that he hoped would have Arizona's 121 death row inmates breaking rocks and digging holes. He said he would work with Corrections Director Sam Lewis to set up the hard-labor program, estimated to begin in 30 to 60 days. "Security is an obvious problem, because we are dealing with the most ruthless killers in the world, who have nothing to lose," Symington said. "But if we can devise a means of doing it, residents of Arizona's death row are going to start digging holes and breaking rocks while their appeals are pending. The work would be done within prison walls. Inmates who refuse will be denied such privileges as television and phone calls."

James Hamm, a murderer who was released on parole, attended law school at Arizona State University and is now an attorney, questioned whether the inmates could be forced to work. "The penalty for those people sitting on death row is execution," he said. "The state has the responsibility for keeping these people until the punishment can be carried out. The law doesn't say they will be sentenced to hard labor until they're executed."

Governor Symington took a different view. On July 14, 1995, he stated: "If the courts want to allow them 10 to 20 years appealing their sentences, that's up to the courts, but how they spend those 20 years is up to the state." He vowed that the death row inmates would not be allowed to sit in their cells just watching TV or in the law library filing endless appeals.

The death row prisoners were to work in the fields planting, weeding and picking vegetables for the prisoners' meals.

The director of corrections, Sam Lewis, retired the day before the chain gang went into effect. It was said that in order to get Lewis to implement this chain gang, a deal was made where Lewis would get to hand pick his successor. The man who replaced Lewis as director was Terry Stewart. When asked about his philosophy of prison management, he said that he believes in "incapacitation." In this model, rehabilitation is not considered, only punishment and keeping the prisoners locked in their cages most of the time. That penal philosophy incapacitates the prisoner so that little violence can occur.

On December 7, 1995, the death row chain gang began. I went out the next day. At 6:30 a.m., an army of police came to our cells with belly chains, leg irons and video cameras. We were made to put on white uniforms that had two thick orange stripes running up and down alongside large black stenciled letters 'A.D.C.' (Arizona Department of Corrections). There were 20 men to a chain gang. We were marched within the prison grounds past yards of general population prisoners who were standing around to see the show. On the tops of the prison walls were numerous police with their Mini-14 rifles (equivalent to a military M-16) trained on us. Once outside the walls we were led along like cattle by three police officers on horseback with shotguns, three pick-up trucks with shotguns and three police officers on foot. After about a mile walking in leg irons with our hands cuffed to our belly chains we reached the fields. Our hands were un-cuffed and we were read the riot act. Four orange traffic cones were placed on the field and we were instructed not to wander beyond them or we would be shot. We were given hoes and rakes with instructions on how to use them to weed out the rows of spinach and cabbage. Each hour we received a short rest break and water. For lunch we had baloney sandwiches and peanut butter and jelly sandwiches along with a Kool-Aid drink. We were given 30 minutes to eat our lunch. We worked for eight hours. We were sweating heavily, and it only reached 80°F. In the summer the average temperatures are 100 to 117 degrees. The sun really bakes and sunstrokes were common.

Later that night and most of the next day, numerous officers asked me what I thought of the chain gang. It took a while to sort out my feelings. The work was hard, but not too difficult. I did not mind it, but I thought of how it would be in a few months when the summer came around. I guessed we would be collapsing left and right. Then the feeling of humiliation came over me, of being marched around in our white uniforms with bright orange stripes on the sides, stumbling as we stepped along with armed guards all around us. I had thoughts of the prisoners in all those concentration camps during the war. Like them, we surely were a ragtag collection of unwanted human beings. I also thought of the southern slaves, bought and sold into hard labor. Our ticket to the same lifestyle was committing a crime. There was no release for the slave but the grave, the same holds true for us. The slaves, however, did not have to work in leg irons.

The story released to the newspapers and news media was that the death row prisoners were going to be put to work growing vegetables in the garden so as to contribute to the welfare of all the prisoners and to help pay our costs of confinement, along with saving the state $175,000 per year as well. They went on to say that the ten cents per hour that they were paying us would enrich our existence and help us to be self-sufficient. The real reason they were paying ten cents per hour was so that the state could not be found guilty of slave labor.

Besides the humiliation of being forced to work on a punishment labor detail such as that, when the police came at 6 a.m. in the morning to the cell, the prisoner had to strip naked, bend and spread his cheeks, lift his testicles, open his mouth and on and on until they were convinced he had no weapons on him. When he finished with the day's work, he had to go through the same procedure before being allowed to return to the cellblock.

Those who refused to leave their cells for the work detail were pepper-maced, then attacked by guards in vast numbers and beaten into submission. They received disciplinary write-ups. They were then dragged out to the work site and required to participate. If they again refused to work, they were placed in a cage the size of a telephone booth made out of chain-link fencing. There was no protection from the hot sun and no room to lie down, so they stood in one spot on their feet all day. A few hours later they were asked again if they would work. If they again answered no they were informed that they were receiving another write-up for disobeying a direct order. They would eventually be brought to disciplinary court and found guilty. They would then lose their privileges for 30 days. That happened each time they refused to work.

There was another agenda here, silent but deadly. For years the death row prisoners had been housed around each other but separated. Security was so tight that when men got mad at each other they could not physically address the problem. When the death row prisoners were put outside on the chain gang with their legs shackled and their handcuffs removed, and were given rakes and hoes to work with, old grudges were soon addressed in a physical manner. Years of pent-up anger and frustration could finally be resolved.

It was inevitable that fights among the prisoners would break out, and they did. There were at least 18 such incidents of prisoner on prisoner violence with and without tools. Each time, the guards would holler out to halt the fighting. When the combatants did not stop, they were fired upon with shotguns. Many prisoners were hit with buckshot or beanbags. Some went to the hospital for treatment. The guards would snicker among themselves about which prisoner kicked another prisoner's ass. They enjoyed it.

On July 5, 1996, a general population inmate working on a chain gang alongside the highway in Tucson was struck by a hit-and-run driver and later died. No arrests were ever made in this crime.

Then on July 10, 1997 it all came to a violent and abrupt end. As usual, a death row chain gang was out in the fields laboring in the morning sun. No one knew that one of the prisoners, Floyd Thornton, was going to make his move and try to escape. Floyd had been corresponding with a woman in the state of Washington. She had moved to Florence, Arizona, where the prison is located and married Floyd just six months earlier. They were married on January 17, 1997.

The fields where we worked were not hidden in the back woods or concealed. The area was right out in the open, at a corner of the prison yard, with only chain-link fencing to secure it from the public roadway. Two major roadways pass on each corner. Anyone could drive up, sit in their car and watch the work going on. That is precisely what Floyd's wife, Rebecca, did. When she spotted Floyd working on the crew, she drove up and parked her car alongside the fence. She leaned over and rolled down the passenger window and picked up an AK-47 assault rifle and began firing off rounds in the direction of the prison guards. Floyd had smuggled a razor in order to cut the leather strap that held the leg chains in place, so was able to run without being hog-tied. During the commotion of the shots being fired, Floyd began to run toward the fence. The officers started shooting at Floyd. He was hit at least two times, but he got up and continued. The rifle Rebecca was firing jammed, so she got out of the car and started firing a .41 caliber pistol. There came a point when Floyd realized he would not be able to make it over the fence, that his escape plan was doomed. He certainly did not want to spend any more time in prison, so he yelled out to Rebecca to shoot him.

Floyd yelled at least three times for Rebecca to shoot him before she finally did. She fired one shot that went right through him. Almost instantly, the police all fired at Rebecca and she went down dead. Floyd died on the way to the hospital. The chain gang was discontinued. We were told that it would return when proper security measures could be put into effect to avoid another catastrophe. Two months later, the entire death row population was moved to the new Special Management Unit II control unit and the chain gang idea was abandoned.

Control units

Control units are the scourge of the American prison system. These units represent the American gulag at its repressive best. In reality, control units reinforce the basic fact that they no longer consider rehabilitation a viable alternative to warehousing. They have given up on the individual and build these repressive concrete tombs to isolate him and destroy his spirit and mind. To break the individual into submission. Few can come out whole. Most either become institutionalized or go crazy in the process.

Most people in society have never heard of a control unit, nor do they care. Control units are buried deep within the prison system. Few people get to see them. Those who know about them do so because they visit a friend or a loved one who is housed in such a unit. If people in the free world were to personally experience the pain and suffering, the isolation, the fear, the sensory deprivation, the lack of human touch, the lack of stimulus, the anger, the psychological warfare, the torture, the smell of death all around, the disrespect, the lack of competent medical services, the paranoia and mental illness, the guards' belligerent macho attitude accompanied by sadism, perhaps changes might be made. None of this is an exaggeration. If anything, I am understating what goes on here.

In the 1800s, solitary confinement was used in American prisons until it became evident that the prisoners in isolation suffered mental breakdowns. Soon after this was discovered, the practice of isolation was abandoned. In response to the turbulent years of the civil rights movement, the massive protests against the Vietnam War and the movement for prisoner's rights, control units were born. Illinois, with the Federal Prison at Marion, and the State of California were the first to build modern control units. Marion went on permanent lock-down status in 1974. Next came the Federal Control Unit at Florence, Colorado.

Although control units cost vastly larger sums of money to build, advocates point to the total control of the prisoners as well as the much lower ratio of staff members to prisoner needed to operate these units. For example, one officer in the control tower and one officer on the floor can effectively supervise 60 prisoners in each of the two death row clusters here in Florence, Arizona. Such low staff numbers make for economic efficiency, which is a huge selling point for the rapid proliferation of control units. There are 57 such prison units across the country at the time of writing. There are two control units in Arizona now, with a third planned. Eventually most of the new prisons will be super-max control units like SMU II.

Numerous experts and studies have shown again today the detrimental effects of sensory deprivation caused by long-term placement in control units. Corrections departments counter by stating that most of those assigned to control units can work their way into lower custody units and thus reduce the negative impact. But we death row prisoners are placed here permanently until we are executed. This clearly shows that we are considered hopeless and not worthy of redemption.

Control units are also used as a dumping ground for the mentally ill. At SMU II, a unit with 120 beds is used for the severely mentally ill. Many of these prisoners are prone to self-mutilation and smearing feces on themselves and the walls of their cells. But they need not be mentally ill to suffer problems in a control unit. About a quarter of all death row prisoners here are on mind-altering medication prescribed by the psychiatrist. Many experience hallucinations and feelings of impending doom. The walls seem to close in on them. They see and hear things that don't exist. Their ears perk up at noises no one else can hear, or when power tools are being used by the staff and they do not know what is going on. As in a zoo, the animals are curious about their cages. Their minds work overtime and it can drive anyone crazy, literally. They can hear the voices of other prisoners and officers, but cannot see them. The cell looks out upon a gray concrete wall. The only time they see another person is when an officer passes by to do a count or serve a meal, or when they are taken out of their cell for a shower, or transported to the medical or counselor's office. They must be strong to adjust to a solitary existence. They long for a human touch, so much so that even the touch of the officers, when they place handcuffs and restraints on them, is welcomed.

Since many general population prisoners will do all their remaining time in control units, and will not work their way to lower custody, when they are released they are like mad dogs who have been caged for too long and shown no affection. Released into society without benefit of a halfway house or counseling, the result is a bitter and dangerous individual. When a person has been forced to survive the environment of a control unit, with its severe deprivations and psychological strain, it is no wonder that it is not long before something triggers a violent eruption causing a regrettable incident, resulting in a return to the criminal justice system or worse. Society and the prisoner both lose.

I have been in various levels of custody in prison, and I can assure you that these control units are a cancer on society, growing at an alarming rate. The public shoulders a large share of the responsibility for them because it seems that all society cares about is that the criminals are taken off the streets and kept off the streets. They entrust all this to the State Department of Corrections, a misnomer because no corrections actually take place in prison, only punishment and violence. Control units are like little islands that society envisions sending all its "bad" members to in order to get rid of them. The power and authority entrusted to the police and the corrections department is slowly but surely encroaching upon society's rights. But for decades now, society has been following the notion that in order to have increased safety, it must sacrifice some of its rights.

A NEW ROUND OF PUNISHMENT

On September 2, 1997, the shakedown crews came into every death row cell and stripped them clean, including even the clothes on our backs. We were given bright orange jumpsuits to put on. No one would tell us what was going on, but we quickly figured out that we were going to be shipped off to SMU II. This was the new control unit in the neighboring Eyman complex where gang affiliates and incorrigibles were kept.

The next day it happened. We were rounded up and taken eight at a time to vans. There was a tremendous show of force and machismo. We were cuffed behind our backs and led through a gauntlet of armed police. When we were loaded on the van we were told that there would be zero tolerance. They would mace us if anything at all happened. Outside the gates there were at least 20 police vehicles, K-9 units, etc. Along the way, there were numerous detachments of Department of Public Safety vehicles and the police who were assigned to intersections were armed with machine guns. There was even a Department of Public Safety helicopter circling above.

When we got to SMU II, we were shoved around like sacks of potatoes. They took the eyeglasses off of our faces (we did not get them back for four days) and with a cop on each arm, we were hurried inside. Once inside, we were pushed into five by five feet rooms. Through a window, I was told to undress, run my hands through my hair, open my mouth, raise my arms, lift my nuts and penis, turn around and spread my cheeks and squat, and then show the bottom of my feet. I was then given a different bright orange jumpsuit to put on. My boots were taken and never returned. Then I was cuffed from behind and rudely pulled out of the room. I was made to walk a long distance in my stockinged feet and up a steel grated stairway to my new cell. My feet were hurting. It took a week to get a change of underwear and a cheap $2 pair of deck shoes—made in China, most likely by prisoners. It took over two weeks to get my property. I succeeded in getting my legal boxes, but a lot of items were missing. They went through every sheet of paper and removed all the staples and paper clips as well as the little brass clips on the manila envelopes.

When I finally did get some of my property returned, I was not permitted to have my stereo, my reading lamp, my hair dryer, my hot pot, my typewriter, my art work, my hobbycraft supplies, my pens and pencils. All those items were considered contraband at SMU II for security reasons. I received my TV and some personal files. That was it.

In addition to all this, the administration has kept promulgating new petty rules and regulations. We are told when to eat, when to get dressed, when to shower and when to sleep. We must get completely naked and go through a body search each time we leave our cells for any reason.

Each officer is a trained observer. They surreptitiously eyeball us and our cells as they pass by. Any minor deviation in our attitudes or mannerisms is noted. It is psychological warfare. Things are done intentionally to unnerve us. There are certain officers who enjoy looking at naked men's bodies. I suppose they are latent homosexuals. One of these officers has the nickname of "Rump Ranger" and another is called "Booty Bandit." Even their fellow officers joke about it.

The chain gang again

We had already been punished by being moved to the control unit. But this was not enough. Suddenly, and without a real explanation, the chain gang was started again. We were told by many cops that since a lawsuit challenging the control unit conditions was put in, and one of the claims was that we were not getting enough exercise, they would give us more exercise! At CB6, we had had six hours a week of exercise, here we got three. This of course was a red herring. The reason was simply punishment. There is no limit to their vindictiveness.

On March 1, 2000, at 6:00 a.m., a platoon of guards came

into our pod. We could hear the belly chains and leg irons as they were being dragged along the floor. We were promptly told that the death row chain gang was being restarted. Five men out of the ten in this pod were told to get naked and they were searched. After which they were handed clothes to put on. Belly chains were put around the men's waist and their hands were placed into handcuffs that were permanently attached to the belly chain. Once out of their cells, leg irons were placed on their ankles. The length of the chain between the two legs was about 12 inches. This length was shorter than the leg irons that were used for the first chain gang at CB6. I mention this because with such a short chain between our legs, it was impossible to take normal strides. When we were hobbled like this, we walked around like penguins. Hopping along is not comfortable. We worked the whole day in these restraints. By the end of the day our ankles were aching. That went on for eight hours each day.

There were ten men per chain gang. We were told a new garden was to be constructed on the prison grounds. Unlike the garden in CB6, the general public could not see what is going on because the field is deep inside the prison itself, and no outsider is allowed on the prison grounds. Abuses could not be observed. We were totally isolated.

The first task we were asked to do was to erect a 100-yard long chain-link fence to close in the work area. Although this is the desert, the ground is not loose sand, but hard, like concrete. It is called "caliche" and is a thick crust of calcium carbonate that forms on the stony soil of arid regions. It took ten men three weeks to dig 20 holes three feet deep for the fence posts.

Those who were not digging the holes were given sledgehammers and told to break up a large concrete platform to make more room for planting, not that much could grow in this barren wasteland.

The officers stood along the fence with their shotguns at the ready. Only one unarmed officer was inside the field area, and he stood far away from the work crew. He called out his orders long distance. The officers knew how much resentment had built up inside the prisoners over the years. They realized how dangerous it would be to allow a prisoner to get close enough to them.

When the new chain gang started, not one TV station in this state and only one newspaper picked up the story. That was, until there was an incident. A short article by Mike McCloy in the *Arizona Republic*, which appeared on May 16, 2000, read as follows:

> Prison officers in Florence slightly wounded two death-row inmates with a shotgun blast Tuesday when pepper spray failed to break up a fight between two chain-gang prisoners. "David Ramirez and Angel Medrano were struck by a few pellets but not injured seriously," Department of Corrections spokesman Michael Arra said. "This will not exempt them from their work requirement. They'll obviously be on separate crews."
>
> Ramirez was convicted of fatally stabbing a Phoenix woman and her teenage daughter in 1989. Medrano was sentenced to die for a 1987 sexual assault and murder of a Tucson woman.
>
> The two inmates were involved in a similar fight in 1996. That incident was the fourth time guards used shotguns to break up fights since the death-row chain gang was started in 1995.

> Chain-gang work for death-row inmates was temporarily halted in 1997 when Rebecca Thornton tried to free her husband, Floyd. As they were caught, she shot him to death at his request, and corrections officers killed her.
>
> "About 98 of Arizona's 117 condemned inmates tend a vegetable garden at the high-security Eyman Complex, rotating in crews," Arra said.
>
> "It sounds like they need to look at their records and keep those two guys separated," said House Judiciary Committee Chairwoman, Marily Jarrett, R-Mesa.
>
> Arra said, "Staff has obviously changed since then. And that is being looked at."

Although the Arizona Department of Corrections had no plans to end this punishment detail, other, unforeseen events dictated otherwise. The effects of the economic recession hit the state severely causing huge budgetary shortages. Estimates of the deficit ran from $250 million to $1 billion. The governor had to make choices as to where to cut funding. The corrections department was not exempt. The department, which was faced with manpower shortages and personnel layoffs, had a meeting on November 29, 2001, and it was decided that the death row hard-labor crew (the chain gang) would be discontinued due to the severe lack of resources. Thus this draconian practice to mete out punishment came to an end, but regretfully for pragmatic concerns of money, rather than humanitarian concerns.

At the time of writing, 2004, Arizona is facing a crisis of lack of prison beds as a result of the "get tough on crime" policies of the past 25 years. When I entered the prison system in 1983, there were only a few thousand prisoners in the state. Now the population has ballooned to 33,000 and is still growing at a rate of 1,000 per year. The state prison system currently has a capacity of 26,000. In order to accommodate the extra 7,000, some prisoners are housed in tents, day rooms, hallways and any place a mattress can be thrown.

Governor Napolitano (who took over from Jane Hull, who had replaced Fife Symington) has a budget deficit of a $250 million to deal with, and it is projected to reach $1 billion by next year. A special session of the legislature was called to deal with the beds crisis. As a stopgap measure they approved an emergency outlay of $27 million for the cost of additional bed space in prisons in Texas and Oklahoma from a private prison firm owned and managed by the now former director of the Arizona Department of Corrections, Terry Stewart. A new prison expansion program totaling $700 million, which will provide an additional 9,100 beds, is planned. The politicians have failed to come up with any fresh ideas to resolve the space problem. Instead they continue to rely upon the "brick and mortar" failed policies of the past.

There may come a time when reasonable heads will seek alternatives. The "tough on crime" policy may need to yield to "smart on crime."

When such large sums of money are dedicated to maintaining and expanding the prison industrial complex, funds must be severely reduced from other areas of the budget such as education. The cost of college tuition has increased drastically over the last decade. The allocation of funds for prisons has increased from 4.3 percent of the state budget to 10.7 percent while higher education has dropped from 19.1 percent to 12.4 percent. One must ask which is more important, the education of our children or the non-rehabitational warehousing of our prisoners? Do we want to spend more money per capita on prisons or on schools?

We are sending more and more people to prison for longer and longer sentences with no effort to rehabilitate them for when they do get released. The "tough on crime" experiment has been a colossal, expensive failure. Arizona was one of the first states to jump on the bandwagon in adopting "truth in sentencing" and "mandatory minimum" guidelines which were designed to eliminate parole. Arizona's sentencing laws are harsher than most states, although statistics show that only 10 percent of Arizona's prison population are classified as violent repeat offenders. Most prisoners are serving time for non-violent crimes and 77 percent are first time offenders. There are 5,300 prisoners serving time for non-violent drug offenses, which equals 22 percent of the total prison population. There are better ways to deal with drug possession convictions and they would free up 5,300 beds.

Another area where changes could improve things concerns elderly prisoners. Statistics from the National Center for Institutions and Alternatives shows that it costs three times as much to house elderly prisoners than younger ones. Arizona has 1,200 prisoners over 55 years old. That age group is known to be less likely to indulge in criminal behavior. These 1,200 prisoners are costing the state the equivalent of some 3,500 younger prisoners. That is a difference of 2,300 beds.

Although parole no longer exists for most prisoners, the older prisoners and some released ex-prisoners are still subject to parole under the old laws. In 2001, 3,267 parolees were returned to prison for technical parole violations—that is, not for new crimes. Parole costs the state $2 per day per person while incarceration costs $55 per day. Which is more cost effective?

Under mandatory sentencing guidelines the judges have little discretion in selecting the most appropriate sentence to fit the crime and the circumstances. Instead, it is the prosecutors who have all the power. They decide what charges to make, what plea bargains to offer and what sentences to apply. They can offer long sentence plea bargains because the mandatory sentence alternative is even longer. The system is completely out of control. Judges should have more discretion to determine sentencing on a case-by-case basis, particularly in drug and alcohol abuse cases. There are too many people in prison who could be handled better and less expensively by drug treatment and probation.

There are many excellent solutions that have been proposed to alleviate the problem, and most of them have been circulated for a long time. It is time to look at them carefully and rationally. They include such improvements as:

1. The pardons and parole board officials should review the sentences of the non-violent offenders who are not a risk to society and grant paroles more generously in order to open up prison bed space.
2. Judges should be relieved of mandatory sentencing limitations for more appropriate discretionary sentences and to allow concurrent sentencing instead of consecutive.

3. Do away with "truth in sentencing" laws and the requirement that 85 percent of the sentence must be served behind bars. The previous system allowed release after 65 percent of time served for good behavior.
4. Utilize drug treatment programs, probation, house arrest and electronic monitoring for non-violent offenders.

These and other programs would serve society better than destroying prisoners' lives with lengthy, futile, imprisonment sentences.

We cannot legislate morality, but we can legislate with common sense.

Chapter 4

Prison Labor, Rehabilitation, Closure, Volunteers

In the years I have been on death row, I have had the time and opportunity to think about certain concepts regarding prison and punishment. Four of them come immediately to mind: prison labor, rehabilitation, closure and volunteers. The first two of these concern the general prison population rather than death row, since I have already talked about the special form of prison labor which exists for death row prisoners in Arizona, the chain gang, and no one even thinks about trying to "rehabilitate" the condemned. These two concepts highlight the overwhelming problems with prisons today. On the other hand, the concept of "closure," a word that has become very popular in recent years, is specific to the death penalty, as is the concept of volunteering. All four of these concepts are very important, because they reflect society's current attitude toward crime and punishment.

Prison labor

The elimination of prison rehabilitation programs and schooling resulted in a large pool of idle prisoners. This created an available source of labor. It did not take long for history to repeat itself by exploiting these prisoners. Prison labor is being sold to the Free World Industrial Complex as a very cheap alternative to moving factories to third world countries so that US corporations can stay competitive. Prisons advertise in trade journals to attract clients. They offer free space for factories, plus a labor force that is almost 100 percent punctual and can be worked seven days a week. A rent-free facility and a literally captive labor force are hard to pass up. This creates a win-win situation for both the prison and the client. Idle hands are put to work thus reducing prison tension and mischief, and entrepreneurs make large profits.

The Thirteenth Amendment reads: "Neither slavery nor involuntary servitude, except as punishment for crimes whereof the party shall have been duly convicted, shall exist within the US or any place subjected to their jurisdiction." This does not eliminate slavery, it just limits it to convicted criminals.

For years, American society was fueled by the Military Industrial Complex. After World War II, the Cold War was the vehicle that took over to keep the economy steaming ahead. For many years the arms race with Russia kept industrial capacity at a high output. Employment was high. After the Berlin Wall came down and communism died, American industry and the military were forced to scale back drastically, resulting in massive layoffs and a large slowing of the economy. An alternative needed to be found to replace both the lost jobs and the tax revenues to the federal and state governments. Enter the prison industrial complex and the return of the prison slavery system.

* * *

To look at prison labor in the USA, we need to look at the past. In the 18th century, prisoners were kept in total isolation, in separate cells, and had no contact with the other prisoners. All of this changed in the 19th century. In order to provide cheap labor for prison construction, prisoners were put to work in quarries to provide stone for the new prisons. Further along it became popular to harness the labor of prisoners without the bother and expense of paying a living wage. Prisons would lease out convicts to various businessmen. It was very popular and inexpensive for contractors. This proved so successful that free-world business organizations petitioned legislatures to stop this unfair practice that was hurting their profit margins. State legislature did not to want see revenue-producing prisons turned into tax burdens, but strong, organized labor finally won out and the contract labor program ended, except to produce items for use by the state.

In Arizona today, all state agencies must purchase items produced by the prison industries before going to outside vendors, regardless of the fact that most prison-manufactured goods are higher in price and lower in quality. In Texas, death row prisoners were able to work in the prison industry shop sewing garments and uniforms worn by the prison guards. The work program was discontinued when the prison was moved to a more secure and repressive unit.

However in California, CMT Blues is a garment factory located at Donovan State Correctional Facility near San Diego. T-shirts and other items are manufactured for companies such as Lee Jeans, Seattle Cotton Works and others. The popular "Prison Blues" brand of jeans are made in Oregon prison shops and proudly bear the logo "made on the inside to be worn on the outside." Japan is a large customer for these particular jeans. Other companies such as Microsoft, Victoria's Secret, TWA, Starbucks, Chevron and Boeing use prison labor in such capacities as data entry, phone reservations, lingerie, water beds, circuit boards and so on. Prisons are becoming factories with fences around them. Prison laborers do not have unions. Entrepreneurs do not supply health benefits, do not pay workmen's compensation insurance or unemployment insurance. And, unlike manufacturing in a third world country, communication is easy because the language is English. Isn't it ironic that the US decries and condemns the export of prison-made goods from such countries such as China while the Prison Blues brand of jeans is exported to Asia and is competing with Asian sweat-shop manufactured goods? That's even after China agreed to stop exporting its prison-made goods to the US.

When outside sources contract for prison labor, they usually pay higher salaries than the prisons pay the prisoners. The deductions that the prison takes from the prisoners' paychecks are a large source of income for the prison. The so-called "costs of incarceration" deductions help contribute to the construction of even more prison labor camps. In order for the prison industrial complex to prosper, there must be a cycle of self-perpetuation to allow the machine to continue on.

It did not take long to realize that prisons were the answer. With large numbers of unemployed workers, a new phenomenon started to appear. Small communities all over the country were actively campaigning for new prisons to be built there. Whereas in the past there was often fear and resentment of bringing convicts into their back yards, communities now realized there was a huge economic benefit because prisons needed corrections officers, office staff, maintenance personnel along with an entire support system for goods and services. The only drawback was that there were not enough new prisons to go around.

In states where there were high enough crime rates to justify building new prisons, often the states could not afford the expenditure. Only so many municipal bonds could be issued before the interest payment costs became prohibitive. Enter the private sector. Large private security companies such as the Corrections Corporation of America (CCA) and Wackenhut Correction Corporation (WCC) who had been operating private prisons in foreign countries became active in convincing the states that they could build and operate the additional prisons needed (mainly minimum and medium-security prisons) and provide a lower per-diem prisoner cost. This was due in part to the fact that the private prisons were not unionized. Poorly trained and even untrained personnel could be hired. Before long the idea started catching on.

Once big business got involved and shares of CCA and WCC were being traded on the New York Stock Exchange, a new growth industry was created. Ways were needed to maintain the growth in this sector. In order to benefit the construction industry and the architectural community, methods had to be found to guarantee a supply of prisoners. Prison construction cannot be expanded without increasing the supply of these "raw materials." Soon after the "get tough on crime" rhetoric, the defendants were usually offered a plea bargain that would guarantee a lesser prison term. This created judicial economy because the cost of many trials was eliminated. It also filled up the prisons and jails.

Federal "truth in sentencing" laws basically did away with parole. The way the laws are written, the prisoner must serve a minimum of 85 percent of the sentence. Good behavior represented only 15 percent of the sentence and it had to be earned. Gone were the days when a person could serve as little as one third of the sentence. "Truth in sentencing" guaranteed that the federal prison population would grow and those in the system would be there for longer periods of time. Politicians saw it as beneficial and in line with their get tough on crime stance, and the private prison corporations saw it as a way to ensure prison capacity for their growth industry.

However, when you over-incarcerate, you devote a huge percentage of the state's budget for corrections. Sooner or later the bill comes due. The "Three Strikes" laws are examples of this. A third strike (conviction) results in the person getting a life sentence in prison. In California, where such laws have existed since 1984, more than 20 new prisons have been built. To compensate for that cost, the California State University has had only one new campus added and no additions have been made to the University of California system. The corrections budget is enormous. Once the prisons are built, they must be staffed and maintained. It is a constant expense. In many states, corrections are the biggest growth industry. Most people do not realize this fact, and if they did, I do not think they would decide to increase incarceration without considering alternatives such as rehabilitation over the educational needs of society.

Surely society can find a better way to deal with crime? Drug treatment centers and counselors can work. Do we want to continue committing ethnic genocide? Federal Justice Statistics show the tremendously high percentage of blacks and Hispanics that make up the vast majority of the prison population. Most drug offenders get first time mandatory minimum sentences.

By not offering drug treatment and counseling and by eliminating educational opportunities we perpetuate the higher incarceration rate of our minority populations. All of these factors are interrelated. Until we acknowledge this vicious cycle, the prison industrial complex will keep rolling along and devouring more and more of our country's resources.

REHABILITATION

Rehabilitation programs are practically non-existent in today's prison system. What goes on in prison is warehousing, punishment and revenge. Punishment and revenge exist because society has been convinced by political rhetoric that prisoners must be made to pay the price for a multitude of societal ills as well as for their own crimes. Someone must be made to suffer.

The measure of a country's "wellness" is reflected in the way it treats its prisoners. In America we do not compare well with other countries in this regard. The mistreatment of prisoners and the increased reliance on executions are rendering our society morally bankrupt. Since we have such a repressive society, with such a punitive penal system, certain psychological needs are developed and maintained. We have effectively established social boundaries between prisoners and society. We place all of our fears and blame all our societal ills on the prisoners and the condemned. In this way, all of the pent up anger and frustrations that exist in society can be "vested" in an acceptable manner, but as a result, our society becomes ill.

Certainly we are not teaching our prisoners a lesson. One of the ways our elected officials in congress and in the individual state legislatures have eliminated rehabilitation programs has been to forbid prisoners to receive Pell Grants, which had been used by prisoners to get an education or learn a trade. This program had been open to all Americans. The yearly grants per person were not high, but even $2,000 or $3,000 could provide a suitable education or vocational program. It was not that the educational programs did not work, they were a huge success. It was learned that giving an individual an education paid for by Pell Grants and prison budgets provided a valuable tool to both the prisoner when he was released and society in general. When a prisoner is empowered with a skill, he is able to integrate back into society and become a productive member. The result is that the recidivism rate drops drastically. Can anyone argue that this is wrong? Most prison administrators supported higher education programs as well because the programs helped to maintain security by keeping the prisoners busy while costing the prison very little. People in prison spend years forging their hopes for the future. Much time was spent in the law libraries learning the law. The educational programs were a symbol of hope that someday you could get out of the criminal justice system. Hope keeps people alive.

However, with all the "get tough" on prisoners sentiment, it was not seen as a good thing to give money to programs for people who are being punished. The appearance of educational programs made many people in society resentful that prisoners could come out of prison better educated than themselves. It appears that society has now given up on a convict having any human worth or value. For the prisoners, the closing of the law libraries and the dismantling of the educational programs have dimmed hopes and returned us to the dark ages.

It is clear that retribution is currently the goal of society, whatever the cost. The shortsightedness of this system will come back to bite us. Since some 90 percent of prisoners will one day be released, if they are not provided with the proper tools to reintegrate, such as an education, they are doomed to failure. When a prisoner is discharged from custody, he is given the clothes on his back and a small amount of "gate" money. In Arizona, it is $50. That does not go far. Everyone knows that, but few care. It is as if society wants the prisoner to fail so that his parole is violated and he is returned to prison in a revolving door scenario. Most people agree that punishment is good, but too much punishment can be counterproductive. The harm created by prison and policies such as the death penalty is not limited to the offender, it also affects spouses, partners, children and other family members. It causes pain and suffering for innocent citizens. They are the unseen victims.

The shift is so far to the right now that we are doing more harm than good. With all the political talk of reinventing government, why are we committed to these old and failed policies? Our reason is that our politicians and lawmakers are stuck in the same paradigm that has been in vogue for over 20 years, the get tough on crime rhetoric. This debate does nothing to address the main issues of society such as drugs, race, education, mental illness, poverty, equal access to jobs and the weakening of the family unit.

There is little evidence that excessive punishment reduces crime, rather there is circumstantial evidence that humiliating prisoners does little to prevent recidivism. People who believe that "fear of the law creates respect for the law" are unrealistic. Society cannot legislate morality. Currently, we are making more laws with harsher penalties and the result is keeping more and more people in prison for much longer periods of time. Specific segments of society are being eliminated.

Increasingly it appears as if we are reverting back to the 19th century, back to the days when we approved of and demanded that people wear the scarlet "A" on their person. Back to a time when we locked people up in wooden yokes and put them on display in the public squares. It was hoped that the public humiliation and the shame that followed would change people's wrongful behavior. But the opposite resulted; people were angry and dehumanized. They became social outcasts—misfits who drew further away from the mainstream, irreparably harmed. When society finally realized the shortcomings of putting people on display and shaming them, and acknowledged that this system did not work, the practice finally ended. But now we have come back to it. Here are some examples:

In Haughton, MA, police captain Richard Pementhal goes on cable access TV and openly denounces and ridicules recently arrested people in the county jail. This is before guilty verdicts have been returned. He has a segment called "Punk of the Week" in which he goes on to shame people by calling them "toilet-licking maggots" and displaying their photos. These people have not yet been to court. What happened to the presumption of innocence? How about defamation of character?

In Houston, Texas, a man convicted of domestic violence was made to stand on the outside stairs of the courthouse and make a public apology as well as being sentenced to shovel horse manure in the police stable for 20 hours a week for six years. Another man was convicted of shoplifting. He was made to wear a sandwich sign that stated: "I Stole From This Store" and pace in front of that store for a period of time. A woman in a similar situation was made to wear a t-shirt saying the same thing, and was to walk in front of a mall shop. We do this in the name of teaching them a lesson so that they will not want to do it again. But is it smart to kick a dog when he is down?

Humiliating people in public is neither productive nor sensible. It is cruel and barbaric. It is not in society's interest to outrage, humiliate and dehumanize in the name of justice. Nothing is gained by shaming the human spirit. It is counter-productive and does not deter crime. It only serves to show the world what a cruel and unforgiving society we have. It is a society that would rather publicly humiliate and execute its citizens instead of attempting to rehabilitate and heal them. While prisoners are paying their debts to society, society is falling deeper into moral debt.

Prevention and educational programs are needed. If we spent just a small portion of the prison construction budget on prevention measures, much benefit would come from it. Instead of huge tax breaks for the wealthy and corporate welfare, we should create tax savings for people and businesses that implement crime prevention measures and reward those who employ ex-prisoners.

We have become a nation of people who do not care about anything except the "self." What happens to others means little. We isolate ourselves from others and only care about our own possessions and our own personal well-being. Whatever has to be done to maintain our own lifestyle is just fine. We have become self-centered and self-righteous. We have not evolved from our basic instincts. We are damaged goods. We see criminals as born-evil sinners upon whom society is justified in wreaking blood vengeance. And this desire to assuage the impulse for vengeance has corrupted the entire criminal justice system. Rehabilitation takes a different mindset. It takes goodwill, time and effort. It says that society cares about the individual enough to try to give them a second chance instead of writing them off. Are we so unforgiving and arrogant that we can just write off so many people as worthless?

In school, history was taught with an emphasis on preventing society from repeating mistakes of the past. We were shown the violent and barbaric nature of man. How terrible it was that the Romans threw their slaves, outcasts and criminals into the lion pit, or pitted men against each other until death. Then there were the Crusades, the religious wars, the World Wars, and so many other crises involving senseless acts of death and violence. So much misery and madness visited upon mankind! Even in times of peace there were hangings, firing squads, and the guillotine. Studying these gruesome examples from the past was to teach us a lesson. Most certainly such teaching was not intended to instill in us a predilection for more bloodletting.

Over the years, very little ever changes in this world. We are all guilty in this society of allowing history to repeat itself. Technology allows us to effectively kill more people than ever before. We use drones, drop laser-guided bombs. It is like one big video game. We lose sight of the fact that we are dealing with human beings like ourselves. As technology becomes more sophisticated, our standards of decency decrease, and our enemies become faceless. However, when it comes to executions, we prefer to relish them in the old-fashioned way.

Why is it that we allow our executions to be a throwback to our more barbaric days? Look at how we execute our prisoners—we hang them, we shoot them, we gas them, we electrocute them and we poison them. Many believe that poisoning by lethal injection is painless; it is not. It appears painless because all the witnesses see is a person going to sleep. Their chest heaves and their lips flap in an unnatural way. Sort of like when you are exhausted and says "phew!" or a raspberry sound, but more extreme and unnatural, involving the entire mouth area instead of just the lips. Of the three drugs used in lethal injection, the first one administered, sodium pentothal, puts the person to sleep. But it is a very short acting barbiturate and the person can recover quickly if any delay occurs in the execution, allowing suffering from the pain of the following drug. Anesthesiologists have testified that the second drug, pancuronium bromide, paralyzes and produces suffocation, which is extremely painful. The doctors stated that when pancuronium bromide is injected the individual has a sudden collapse of the chest and lungs as if an elephant has sat down on him. The final drug, potassium chloride, causes extreme burning. Yet we allow this torture because it gives the false illusion of an easy death. It is a fatal deception.

All this is done in a manner that is ritualistic, almost a show, as I describe in the next chapter. Rehabilitation could not deliver such satisfying entertainment. And, of course, we deserve our pleasure, don't we? We don't want to be cheated of vengeance, we want our full pound of flesh. To make certain of this, we legislate new laws to hasten the demise of those we consider to be "expendable and worthless" members of our society. Oh, we do love our blood sport! If you doubt this, just look at Florida. How many times did "Old Sparky" have to malfunction and produce flaming heads and nose bleeds before it was stopped? Instead of feeling shame for these grotesque displays of cruelty, the politicians remained true to form by feeding on the frenzy of the populace in Florida. They grabbed the spotlight by bragging that these malfunctions possibly awaited anyone who committed murder in their state—that any criminal just might die in a similar excruciatingly horrible and painful manner.

An example is Lee "Tiny" Davis. When he was executed in the Florida electric chair July 8, 1999, he bled so much from the nose that his shirt was covered with large bloodstains. Florida had declared that malfunctions in the past did not signify that the use of "Old Sparky" was a cruel and unusual punishment. Such was the outrage experienced by Florida Supreme Court Justice Leander Shaw at witnessing yet another display of what he construed to be barbaric cruelty, that he publicly posted three photographs of the dead Davis strapped in the electric chair with blood all over his chest as proof of how Davis was brutally tortured to death, so that the public would witness the indecency of it.

People were indeed furious and upset over the posting of the execution photographs, but not for the reasons Shaw intended. It was not because the photos showed such a gross spectacle of a horribly botched execution, rather they were upset because only three photos were posted! They were demanding that more photos be displayed.

The electric chair was finally retired in Florida, and lethal injection added as the execution method. But the addition was made with the utmost reluctance. It was done only because the courts, disagreeing with Florida, were threatening to declare the electric chair "cruel and unusual punishment" and therefore unconstitutional. Since the electric chair was Florida's sole method of execution, the state would have been left with no possibility of carrying out any executions at all.

We've given up on the model of rehabilitation and thus we have learned little from the past. We kill in the name of law and order at the price of forfeiting our decency. After all, someone has to pay for the ills of society. And at the same time, we cannot figure out why our kids are taking guns to school and killing so many of themselves. Certainly we teach our youth through executions that human life has little value and that decency does not matter. We also teach that trying to improve the human condition through rehabilitation is not worth our efforts, so we should just close our eyes to what we don't want to deal with.

Closure

Closure is a very difficult to discuss because the word offers so many different interpretations. It is a hard word, a difficult word, a cruel word. My opinion on this topic may be even harder for some to accept because I am a person who has taken the life of another. It may seem that my words are hollow. I assure you they are not. It would be easier for me not to approach this subject, but I must because of the importance that closure has in the overall discussion of capital punishment in society.

Perhaps the best way for me to deal with this subject is to tell about a closure experience shown in a television program broadcast on *48 Hours* on February 4, 1998, entitled "My Daughter's Killer." I reviewed that program for *The Forum Newsletter*, an abolitionist publication.

The program told the story of Mitzi Ann Nalley, who in 1986 was murdered by Jonathan Wayne Nobles in Austin, Texas. The program revolved around her mother, Paula Kirkland, who—over the protestations of family and friends—struggled to meet face to face with her daughter's killer, two weeks before his execution in 1998. Texas is one of a number of states that have a program where victims of crime and/or their relatives can meet face to face with prisoners in sessions prepared and mediated by prison counselors.

Nalley's murder was gruesome and senseless. Nobles broke into the house through the back door; Mitzi and some girlfriends had returned from celebrating her 21st birthday. She was stabbed 28 times and died. Her boyfriend, Ron Ross, was sleeping in another room. He woke up, and during a struggle in which Nobles himself was cut, Ross was stabbed 19 times. He ran outside the house, where he collapsed. A neighbor called the police. Following the trail of Nobles' blood, police found witnesses who told them that Noble had asked them for bandages and Band-Aids.

Nobles was caught and confessed on tape. He never showed remorse nor took responsibility for the crime, blaming his bad childhood, mental problems and drug abuse. After a month-long trial, the jury took three hours to find him guilty. He received the death penalty.

For many years, Nobles refused to participate in the process that would lead to a face-to-face meeting with Paula Kirkland. During that time, however, Nobles underwent positive changes. He sincerely found religion, overcame his denial and accepted responsibility for his crime. Eventually, he agreed to counseling and to meet with Ms. Kirkland.

A large portion of the program chronicled the pain and suffering that Paula Kirkland went through. A homemade cedar chest served as a shrine to Mitzi; it held memories. Ms. Kirkland stated that she wanted to tell Nobles what he had done to her life, how much suffering and pain he caused during the previous 12 years. Then reconciliation and closure could occur.

One began to suspect her motives of reconciliation and closure when she objected to Nobles' participation in a program that allows prisoners, even on death row, to donate vital organs in return for a reduced sentence. She saw this as a ploy by Nobles to cheat her out of her closure. Worse, by donating organs, parts of Noble would live on in other people, whereas Mitzi is forever lost to the world. Ms. Kirkland felt that this would taunt her and haunt her.

Guard tower, entrance gate and visitation room.
SMU II, Florence, Arizona. (Private archives.)

Outside holding pens. SMU II, Florence, Arizona.
(Perry Kretz/Stern/Picture Press/SOA.)

Corridor at maximum-security prison, Florence, Colorado.
(Stephen Ferry/Getty Images.)

Cover photo, *Tucson Weekly* (J.E. Kelly reporting on the prison in Florence), April 28–May 5 1999. (Private archives.)

Typical cell, Florence, Colorado.

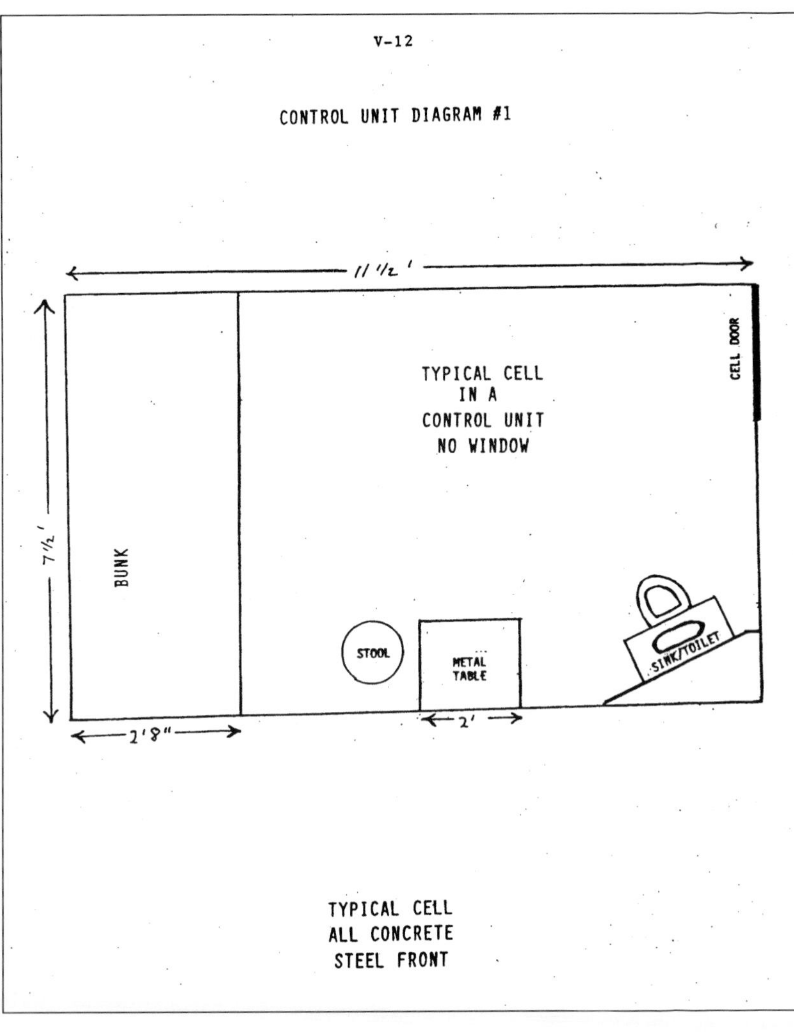
V-12
CONTROL UNIT DIAGRAM #1
11 1/2'
7 1/2'
BUNK
TYPICAL CELL
IN A
CONTROL UNIT
NO WINDOW
CELL DOOR
STOOL
METAL
TABLE
SINK/TOILET
2'8"
2'
TYPICAL CELL
ALL CONCRETE
STEEL FRONT

CONTROL UNIT DIAGRAM #3

SHOWER
BUNK
BUNK
BUNK
BUNK
BUNK
UPPER TIER WALKWAY
OVERHEAD SKYLIGHT
LIGHT ENTERS COMMON AREA ONLY - NOT INTO CELLS
OVERHEAD SKYLIGHT
LIGHT ENTERS COMMON AREA ONLY - NOT INTO CELLS
STAIRWAY UP
UPPER LANDING
EXERCISE AREA DOOR
OUTDOOR EXERCISE AREA
(NO EQUIPMENT)
20'
7'
POD ENTRANCE

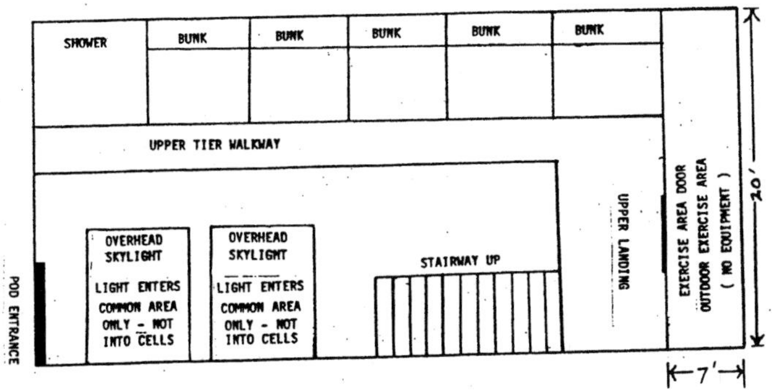

TOP VIEW
CONTROL UNIT
10 MAN POD
WITH EXERCISE ROOM

CONTROL UNIT DIAGRAM #2

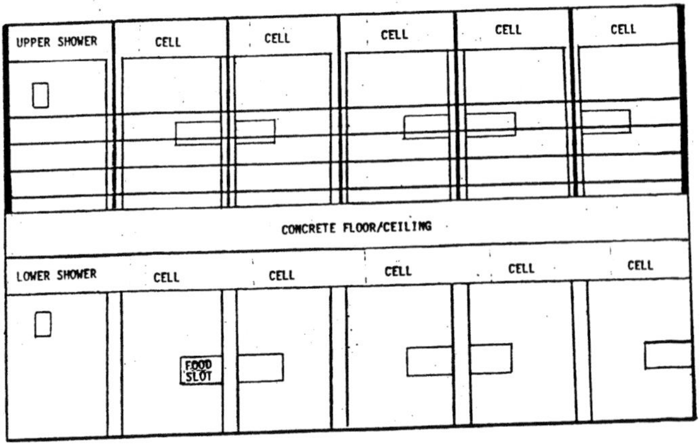

FRONT VIEW
10 MAN POD
5 UPPER/ 5 LOWER CELLS

CONTROL UNIT DIAGRAM #4

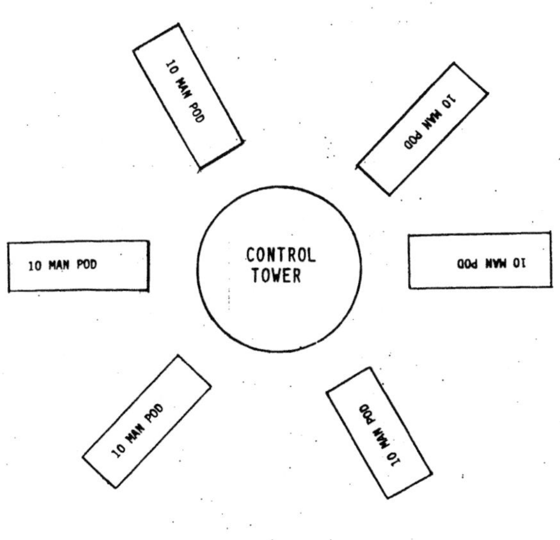

TYPICAL POD CLUSTER
SIX PODS TO A CLUSTER
60 PRISONERS

DAILY NEWS
NEW YORK'S PICTURE NEWSPAPER
EXTRA
EDITION
DEAD!

Execution of Ruth Snyder on the electric chair in Sing Sing.
Daily News, New York, January 12, 1928.
(Private archives.)

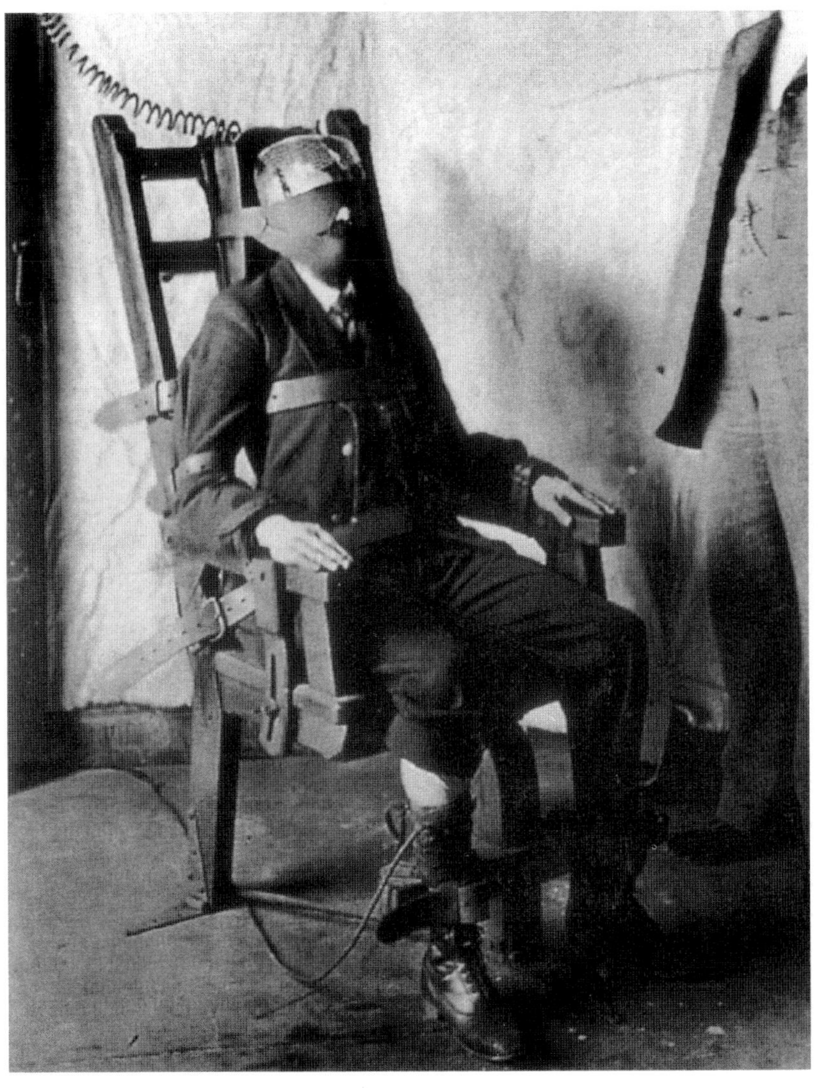

Prisoner awaiting execution, US. September 12, 1908.
(The Granger Collection, New York.)

Hanging of Arthur Gooch, McAlester, Oklahoma, 1930. (Roger Vidlet/Rex.)

Noose from Florence, Arizona. (Arizona Museum.)

Gas Chamber. Florence, Arizona.
(Stern/Picture Press/SOA.)

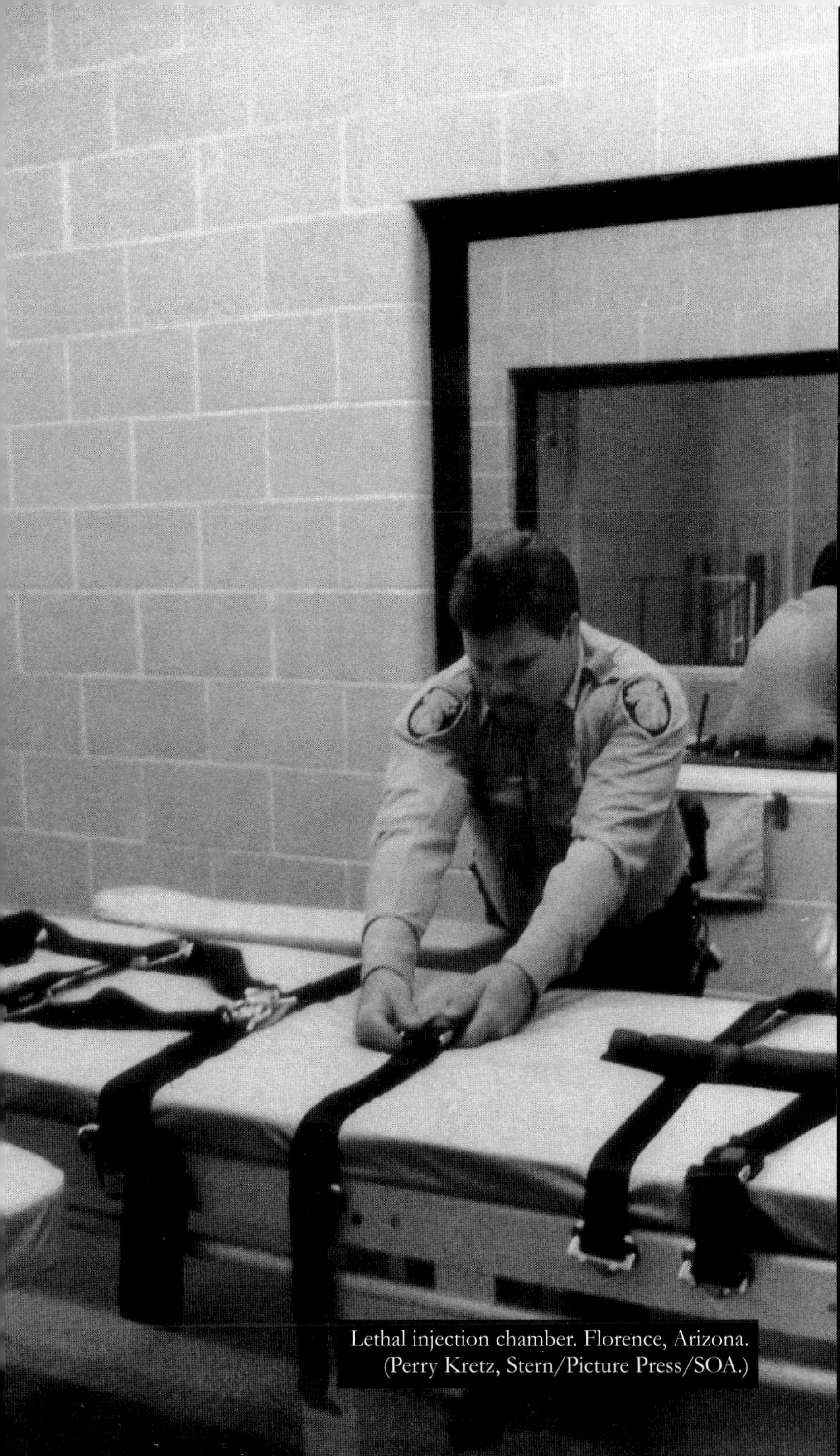

Lethal injection chamber. Florence, Arizona.
(Perry Kretz, Stern/Picture Press/SOA.)

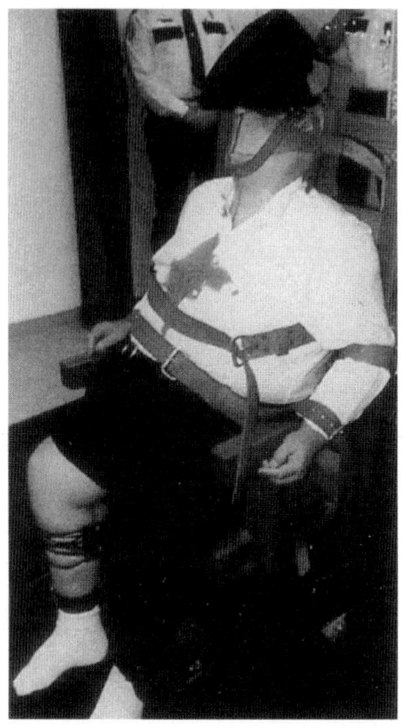

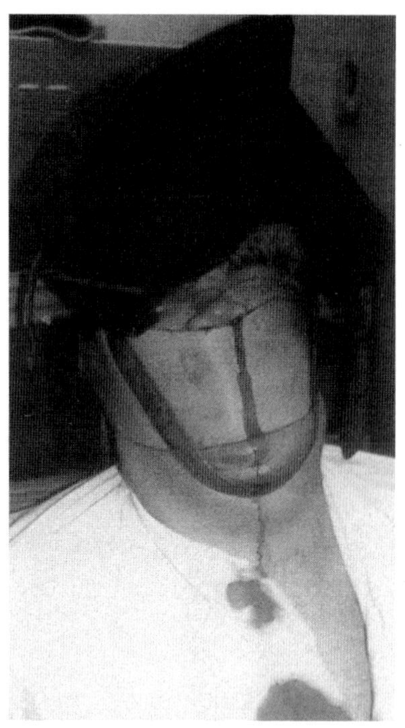

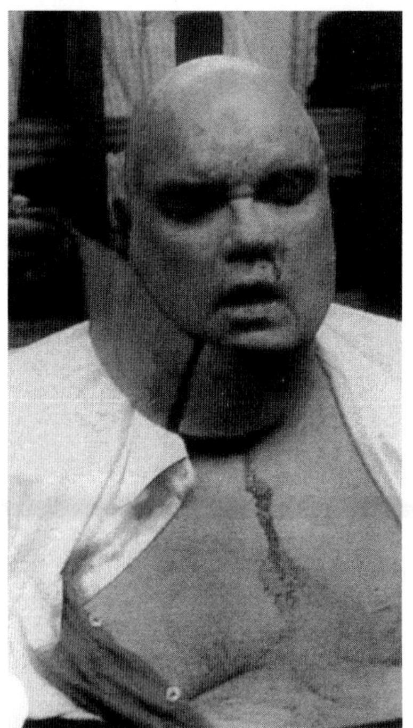

Execution of Allen Lee (Tiny) Davis
on the electric chair,
Florida, July 8, 1999.

The day came when Nobles and Paula Kirkland met face to face. Paula wore a photo of Mitzi on her dress to remind Nobles of his crime. She got a blessing from the prison priest. She loudly told Nobles how he ruined her life and caused her so much pain. Nobles broke down in tears and apologized to her. He acknowledged that he could never comprehend her pain, that death would be easier than this meeting with her. She broke down and they took time out.

The entire meeting took a full day. When she returned, they agreed on how much of a monster he was. Nobles stated that if he could give his life to bring Mitzi back, he would. Ms. Kirkland replied that was not enough. Nobles was still remorseful and agreed that being sorry was not enough, that sorry was cheap after bringing grief into her life, but he had done his best to change. Again, he apologized. Ms. Kirkland could not really forgive him, but she could offer him some forgiveness because her God compelled her to do that much. Forgiveness or not, she told Nobles she still wanted to watch him die.

As the execution day approached, Paula Kirkland stated that she would finally get her life back. But if Nobles did not die, if he got a commutation, then what? Would her obsession for revenge drive her crazy and cause more pain? This was a possibility, because like so many relatives of murdered victims, Paula Kirkland chose to dwell in a reality that has banished all emotions except the rage felt over a past crime. She could not evolve from this; there is no present or future for her unless she drags her pain along with her.

The fact that death row prisoners can come to grips with their crimes and feel genuine remorse did not concern her. A death poisoned her life, perhaps an execution could heal it? But, either way, Mitzi is gone, nothing will fill that void except a conscious effort to let go of crippling emotions and move on. That is something that even prisoners, saddled with the guilt and remorse for their crimes, must learn to do, on top of all the pain and stresses of the death row experience. But some people are unable, or unwilling, and refuse to do it.

Nobles' request to donate organs was turned down. Paula Kirkland then worried that Governor Bush might commute Nobles' death sentence. Of course, he wouldn't. This is Texas, get real! So Ms. Kirkland got her wish to witness Nobles' execution. From his gurney, Nobles told Paula that he loved her and again he apologized for the harm he had done her. Then he started to sing "Silent Night" until the poison flowing into his veins silenced him forever.

After the execution, Ms. Kirkland received an envelope left for her by Nobles. It contained a religious medal. She was shown putting it into the cedar chest that holds Mitzi's memories. But whether Paula Kirkland's rage and pain can be put away as easily as closing that chest's lid is another question. If time dulls her pain, she might learn to see Nobles as something more than an object for revenge. Her God may make her understand that to be forgiven, one must forgive, even as her Lord asked forgiveness for those who nailed him to a cross. Perhaps when Nobles, like Mitzi, becomes a burden of pain and regret in Paula Kirkland's memory, she will force herself to forget and find a better life for herself.

As a death row prisoner, I may be accused of being insensitive to the theory of closure. I plead no contest. In a society that is so fueled by hatred and revenge toward criminals, many relatives of murdered victims are told by prosecutors that they are being disloyal to the person who died if they don't want the murderer to die as well. That it will make them whole again. They are led to expect that the murderer's death is going to help them heal. It doesn't. All it does is make them focus on anger and hatred. After the execution, when all of the focus of their hatred is gone, they are left empty. It does allow them to vent their anger and hatred, and psychologists may argue that this is "healthy" and helpful. But the theory of closure hinges on the illusion of instant healing when the killer breathes his last, and that is not so. Healing is not instantly realized after executions are completed. It comes about through the same effect of will that would have healed relatives' grief years earlier had they not been obsessed with thoughts of revenge and focused on executions as the way to achieve inner peace. So closure is a will-o'-the-wisp, a false and cruel hoax, a lie that almost always results in disappointment and renewed pain.

Nothing ever fills the void left by the death of loved ones, whether the death resulted from murder or from natural causes. The proof of that lies in the fact that relatives of murdered victims often claim that there is no closure for them, even years after the killer of their loved one was executed. Human beings never come to grips with loss, any more than rehabilitated substance abusers ever overcome the craving for drugs or alcohol. Healing, such as it is, such as we are capable of, is ours to the extent that we are not crippled if we wish to move on—exactly what closure seekers never wish to do. That is why forgiveness is so basic to emotional healing; it helps to control the hurtful cravings of hatred and revenge. No one can achieve closure or forgiveness by killing yet another person.

Zen has a number of koans (riddles) which deal with the difficulty of putting aside, letting go, of some emotional obsession. One of the major elements of Buddhism (which is not a religion as much as a philosophical system), is leaving the internal pathway of human passions. Closure could do that in some cases if it were properly carried out. But the stronger the passion to obtain closure, the lower the probability that one will achieve the right pathway.

Those who attend the execution of the person responsible for the death of a loved one will be marked by the experience—that is guaranteed. But if they think retribution will produce closure—that is not likely because evil cannot efface evil. One does not conquer monsters by becoming one.

In this sense, a religious pathway may produce closure, and allow the putting down of a burden that has been carried for years. That is not forgetting (impossible for all), or even forgiving (impossible for some), but a liberating event in which one has removed the burden in some fashion. There are many ways of doing that but they are achieved individually. There is no standard way, and executions are certainly not the "silver bullet."

Psychologically speaking, a powerful part of healthy living is the ability to forgive and the ability to pardon others. We realize that anger is natural, and in order to deal with anger effectively we learn to let go of everyday hurts (pardoning). Few people understand that forgiveness is not excusing, forgetting or denying an offense, and it does not always lead to resolution. It is recognizing that you have been wronged, giving up all the resentment, and responding with compassion. The benefits from this include reduced anxiety and stress, and fewer mental problems. Forgiveness is so strong that it brings the healing that is a necessary element of our humanity. Our inability to forgive can certainly destroy our lives, both individually and collectively, for when we refuse to forgive others, we become the ones who suffer. Forgiveness does not have to be a reconciliation of the two parties, forgiveness only requires one person.

Unfortunately, to most of us on death row the word closure represents vengeance. We live in a bloodthirsty society that demands revenge. Revenge and justice are not the same thing. I know there are many men and women on death row who have reflected upon their crimes over their long years of waiting to die and who would be comforted to be able to reach out to the victims of their crimes and in some cases receive forgiveness. Those who do not believe in forgiveness would simply say that we on the row have nothing coming. We don't deserve compassion. I contend that every human being deserves compassion.

I can speak from experience when it comes to forgiveness. I related in the last chapter how I received an execution warrant scheduling me to die on July 24, 1996. Although I had reason to believe I would receive a stay of execution, the newspapers and the TV picked up on the story and predicted my demise. I eventually did receive a stay before the 24th. I also received a personal letter from one of the victims of my crime. There were two immediate victims, the man who died and a neighbor friend who heard shots and came running into the house. She was shot, but thankfully she survived. This note was hand delivered to me by the deputy warden of the cellblock. Since there are restrictions on communications between prisoners and their victims, the note was delivered in a sealed envelope after having made its way through the proper channels at the Department of Corrections in Phoenix. I was informed that the letter was from a victim of my crime and I was asked if I wished to receive it. Without hesitation, I said yes.

The ironic part of this was that by the time the department had processed the letter and delivered it to me, it was a week after the date I was due to be executed. If I had been executed, I would never have had the opportunity to read it.

The letter was handwritten. It was obviously difficult for her to write to me and she didn't know if I would be receptive to it. After all these years she felt compelled, but afraid to write it. She had learned of my impending execution which was very emotional for her and she said she did not know how to react to it. She explained that the Lord holds us accountable for our actions and we must pay for our sins as well as ask for forgiveness. She closed with the following: "Too many things go unsaid and then it's too late. I wanted you to know that I have forgiven you for your actions against me and hope in some way that this will bring peace to your heart as it also heals mine. God bless you."

I was emotionally rocked after I read this beautiful letter. For years I had wanted to reach out to her but was afraid to do so because of the strict rules about writing to one's victim and because I didn't want to cause her any more pain. It had been 13 years since the crime, and I had long since asked God for forgiveness. Many times I wished I could tell my victims how sorry I was to have inflicted the pain and suffering that was so unnecessary and unwanted. Now the door had been opened. I wrote a long letter which my attorney forwarded to her. I told her what a wonderful person she was to forgive me and expressed my regrets over all the pain and suffering I had caused her, her family and the family of the other victim. That was very cathartic for me.

Over the years, all prisoners on death row have come to experience the bitterness of a society that clamors for more punishment, speedier executions and their share of retribution. More sentences for more crimes, more crimes eligible for the death penalty, longer time in prison for one's crime until most will never get out. Out of sight, out of mind. They feel that prison is the only way to deal with crime because if they release prisoners, they will just commit new crimes. In their eyes, few if any of us are good people and fewer yet are capable of rehabilitation. And the more prisoners we execute, the safer they believe society will become. That is a most tragic commentary on modern society.

If anyone could travel in my shoes, down the roads I have walked during the 20 years that I have been on death row, they would be very surprised. It is not easy to die a little bit each day, to see loved ones pass away and not be able to commiserate with friends and family, to see how we are condemned for all of society's ills. Every individual on this troubled earth deserves to be touched by love, to be accorded the opportunity to express his or her feelings, to be able to touch another human being. Every person has the ability to change—some may not, but those who can should be given the chance. We are not all made of concrete. Feelings of compassion, love, the understanding of right from wrong, can reach us all. We are affected by all that goes on around us. The greater crime is to lump us all together as failures and discard us all on the refuse pile as if we were human waste. We must learn that every person has value and worth and each individual must be judged for who and what he or she is and could become, not what they once may have been. We human beings have the ability to learn, adapt and change. The letter I received from my victim says volumes about love and understanding. She has shown me what a beautiful and wonderful person she is. To reach out to me after some 13 years, on the eve of my execution, and express her forgiveness of me, allows me to have faith that compassion and forgiveness still exist in our world, no matter how limited they are. The politicians, the courts and the judges may not see any redeemable value in me, but the compassion of this one person says it all. We might wish that we could change the past, but since that is impossible, it is the present that confines us and defines us. I must take solace in the knowledge that this letter has healed her heart as well as having brought peace to my own. I regret that the vast majority of death row prisoners will not have the opportunity to experience such fulfillment because of the mindset of our society. Forgiveness does not cost a cent, but it takes a lot of heart.

Volunteers

Although the term "volunteer" has been in vogue for a number of years relating to executions, not everyone makes the correct association. Usually, one would associate the word "volunteer" with someone who gives of him or herself for the benefit of others. However, this same word has also come to be synonymous with any death row prisoner who gives up what is left of his or her appeals and "volunteers" to be executed without delay. It is suicide by cop. The question needs to be asked: does any benefit accrue from such a volunteer? There is no doubt whatsoever that as far as the overwhelming majority of the general public in the USA is concerned, any execution is most certainly perceived as being a beneficial event, regardless of whether it is due to the exhaustion of a prisoner's appeals or the decision to volunteer.

When I came to death row in the early 1980s, there were no executions taking place in Arizona. The prisons were not as crowded as they are now and the political atmosphere both in the state and country as a whole was not as bloodthirsty and right-wing conservative as it is today. Politicians had not yet realized the political rewards stemming from the adoption of "get tough on crime" policies, together with the strategy of advocating the use of the death penalty for the increasing number of crimes that were seen to shock the voters. When I came to the row, there had not been an execution since 1963, when Manuel Silvas was put to death in the gas chamber. So, when Donald Harding suffered the same fate in 1992, a new era was underway.

Twenty-nine years had passed without an execution in Arizona. During those years prisoners were able to win a number of lawsuits challenging the poor prison conditions in the Federal District Court. This, however, did not inhibit the Arizona Department of Corrections (ADOC) from embarking on a "Master Plan" to make life as miserable as possible for all the prisoners in the system. Some of its major elements were confiscation of almost all personal property, even when it was purchased by the prisoner or members of his family; the loss of the right to have Christmas food boxes sent in; closing of the law libraries and elimination of all prisoner legal assistants (jail house lawyers) who assisted others with disciplinary hearings and filing lawsuits; changes in the disciplinary policy to exclude street attorneys from representing prisoners at disciplinary hearings; redesigning of the grievance procedure to eliminate any chance for the prisoner to succeed with it; loss of hobby-craft privileges; the chain gang; and, finally, the transfer of all death row prisoners to the Eyman Complex, Special Management Unit II. The Master Plan was a recipe for despair, and the results of that despair have appeared.

Recently, three Arizona prisoners committed suicide by hanging themselves. A prisoner in Tucson and a man here in the Eyman Complex hung themselves with a sheet and with shoelaces respectively. The third man in the Florence Complex used shoelaces to kill himself. It did not take but a few days for the goon squad to come to our cells and take away all personal tennis shoes. All they really wanted was our shoelaces, but what better opportunity to take the shoes as well! Suicides are not welcomed by the ADOC because they bring unwanted attention to the daily operations of the gulag. They shudder at the thought that someone might investigate why so many people are killing themselves. If people did look into what was going on they would see how living conditions have deteriorated to the point that many prefer suicide to enduring prison life.

Every individual has a breaking point. Depression plays a big part in most prison suicides. The mean-spiritedness of ADOC is a major factor in destroying a human being's will to live. There is no doubt that the majority of these suicide deaths result from the pressure of the circumstances heaped upon us all by the "Master Plan." A further question must be asked: when someone is pushed to suicide, is he or she a "volunteer?"

The state does not want to be seen as the "harbinger of death." This kind of volunteering is not acceptable. But when it comes to a death row prisoner who decides to forego his or her appeals and be executed, the state is more than happy to assist. No shoelaces required! Just say the magic word, "volunteer," and a state-assisted suicide will be provided. After all, this is the fruit of the "Master Plan," when self-sanctioned death becomes more appealing than dying a little more each day on death row.

In this supermax control unit, we are subjected to the harshest conditions in the entire prison system. This is no coincidence, although it was claimed that we were moved here for security reasons. No death row prisoner ever escaped from our previous maximum-security unit at CB6. When some of the death row prisoners filed a lawsuit over the conditions of SMU II, the ADOC and SMU II administrations claimed that they were unaware that we were being denied rights and privileges that we had been afforded at CB6.

When someone volunteers, I think little attention is paid to that person's mental condition. There is the obligatory psych review by the prison psychiatrist, but not many fail that. Yet the very fact that someone volunteers to be killed should raise a red flag indicating a need for extensive psychiatric tests. Many death row prisoners have undiagnosed mental disorders and psychoses. Proper treatment of these disorders might change a volunteer's decision to choose to die. But this would go against the execution protocol.

Under the new restrictive policies, the first three death row prisoners to volunteer for a state-assisted suicide were John Brewer, Darren Bolten, and Arthur Ross. One has to assume that these three men were not perceived as having any value, and that therefore they were allowed a state-assisted suicide even though they enjoyed perfect health. Dying citizens in the free world, no matter how poor their health or how great their pain, would be denied such assistance. Euthanasia is frowned upon by society. Life is considered too valuable to allow death on demand.

On November 8, 2000, the fourth volunteer, Donald J. Miller, was executed here by lethal injection. I knew Donald from the first day he arrived on death row. Over the years he suffered from depression and was mildly retarded. When we were moved to this control unit, he rapidly went downhill mentally. It was too painful for him to endure, so he dropped his appeals and volunteered to be executed.

Since he still had his Federal appeals left, he was assigned an attorney from the Federal Public Defender's Office to assist him. This attorney, Dale Baich, is the same attorney I have and he is a very capable and caring man. He had to get a court order to visit Miller in prison. The court granted visitation and unlimited phone calls to Miller. After the first visit, Dale was barred by the ADOC from returning to visit Miller a second time. Deputy Warden, David Cluff, and the Director of Department of Corrections, Terry Stewart, both insisted that "visitation" meant only one visit, that the court did not say unlimited visits. Unbelievable! Dale Baich had to go back to the Federal Judge and get a new order. The court was upset that the ADOC would try to limit attorney-client visits, especially when the client was a few days away from death! The court made it clear that Miller could see his attorney as much as he wanted to up until his death.

The previous year there had been seven executions in Arizona, whereas in 2000 there had only been two executions before Miller. It is appalling that the ADOC would try to limit the attorney visits of a man just before his death. But the ADOC was worried that, by speaking with his attorney, Miller might be persuaded to continue his appeal process and stop the execution. Obviously, once the machinery of death tastes of blood, it keeps rolling on, resisting any attempt to deny it fresh bodies.

The premise that everyone on death row represents the dregs of society is sadly incorrect. That is because the death penalty is unfairly administered. Forget the aggravating and mitigating circumstances—what really counts are the outside influences and politics involved.

Although only a small percentage of prisoners receive the death penalty, the majority of those who are sentenced to death are guilty of having insufficient funds to pay for a competent attorney. Consequently, an overworked and underpaid public defender or a contract attorney is appointed to represent the indigent defendant. There is truth in the comment that has been made concerning capital punishment, "if you have the capital, you don't get the punishment!"

There are many cases that clearly demonstrate the inequity in sentencing where mass murderers are spared the death penalty. There was a major case in Arizona called "The Temple Murders," in which two young men killed seven Buddhist monks in a temple and stole their money and valuables. That was felony murder for pecuniary gain, but the culprits received life sentences. In 2003, in Washington state, the "Green River" murderer killed over 48 women over two decades and received a life sentence. Gary L. Ridgeway, confessed to having sex with the prostitutes and runaways, murdering 48 women then driving around to dump their bodies. The state agreed to a life sentence in order to get Ridgeway's cooperation in locating the bodies.

At the court hearing, Ridgeway made the following statement:

> I killed 48 women. In most cases I did not know their names. Most of the time I killed them the first time I met them and I do not have a good memory for their faces. I killed so many, I have a hard time keeping them straight. I placed most of their bodies in groups, which I called, "clusters." I did this because I wanted to keep track of all the women I had killed. I liked to drive by the clusters around the country and think about the women I had placed there.

Gary Ridgeway ranked right along with such killers as Jeffrey Dahmer and Charles Manson. Heinous killers like them are exactly the ones who the death penalty was envisioned to be for, but they did not get the death penalty. Whereas a robbery gone bad, where one person is killed, often results in a death sentence. If that is not an inappropriate application of the death penalty, what is? Death for the "worst of the worst" killers is not the norm. Those who get the death penalty are the poor who cannot afford a quality defense team. Those who can afford quality representation get life sentences.

It is estimated that death penalty cases cost the state between $1 million and $7 million dollars for each case, whereas cases that seek life sentences average $500,000.

At the time of writing there have been 113 innocent persons released from death sentences. In Arizona recently, Ray Krone was released after DNA evidence exonerated him. Proponents of the death penalty often claim that there is no proof that any innocent person has been executed. With 914 executions since 1977, the 113 exonerations represent an error rate of 12.5 percent. This suggests that up to one in eight of those executed may have been innocent. Usually when someone is executed the case evidence is destroyed and the case dies along with the condemned. It is impossible to prove innocence after that.

I used to think that any prisoner who would give up his or her appeals and consent to a state-assisted suicide had to be a very troubled or weak person. There are still a lot of men on the row who think this, who look upon volunteers as weak because they do not stand strong and are always complaining about the conditions. They believe that volunteering saves the state lots of money that can be then used against other death row prisoners to kill them faster. And it is true that volunteering saves money by reducing the court calendar, allowing the state to concentrate more on the others.

However, since the "Master Plan" began to tighten the screws on every aspect of life in prison, I no longer feel the same about volunteers. Since everyone has a limit, the worse conditions become, the more volunteers will step up to check out. I cannot fault someone who has had enough of this pain and madness, enough of the depression and desperation. My only regret is that every time someone volunteers to be put to death, it inadvertently sends a message to the state attorney general and ADOC that their "Master Plan" is working well. They are reaping the fruits of their labor, and can derive a perverse pleasure and satisfaction from their sadism.

Considering how poor conditions are in prisons today all over the country, and since ways will certainly be found to make them harsher still, it is imperative that some of our friends in the abolitionist movement understand the fundamental problem of life in prison. I have heard many men on the row say they are convinced there is no hell after death because this life is the real hell. No one in prison wants to live longer under the current conditions. The Death Penalty Information Center and Amnesty International believe that conditions in Oklahoma's H-Unit, an underground death row building, has increased the number of volunteers there. The percentage of volunteers is now 36 percent. Choosing when one dies is one of the few things a death row prisoner can control.

Lately there has been a movement to push for Life Without Parole (LWOP) as a substitute for executions. Some abolitionists have even supported this movement. But there are very few death row prisoners who favor that as a solution. If they could walk in our shoes, they would learn that the last thing we want is to be abandoned and left to die a slow and painful death with this unnatural "natural life." Prison is hell, plain and simple. At least with the death penalty, there is a finite end to this suffering. Furthermore, if the LWOP movement succeeds, we will become forgotten. We will no longer have a forum—the issue is lost.

Previously, the alternative to the death penalty was life in prison without parole for 25 years. Although a quarter of a century in prison is a long time, it still allows for hope. Hope allows for change and reduces the idleness, abuse, neglect and thoughts of revenge. Where there is hope, there is life.

Those who have not been in prison do not often think of growing old behind bars. However, the fastest growing segment of the prison population is the elderly. With medical treatment in prison being minimal at best, the rate of detection and early treatment of serious problems is very poor. Thus growing old in prison and dying in prison, and especially living and dying in pain, is a crueler fate than a quick execution. It is an alternative form of the death penalty.

Add to this prison policies of incapacitation, punishment and revenge and the total loss of hope that accompanies a sentence of Life Without Parole, and you have a prison population that has nothing to look forward to or live for. No one desires to die old, lonely and sick in prison.

However, this is an alarming new trend. There are over 3,700 people on death row, but there are more than 20,000 people who are serving LWOP. When society locks the door and throws away the key it signifies a belief that there is little or no value in human life. If we are a Christian society, as we like to think we are, what has happened to the belief that there is God in every person, that good can be found in everyone, that each individual is a person of worth and value deserving of being treated with respect and humanity regardless of the crimes committed, or behavior towards others? Is it not a bigger crime to give up on humanity and just write prisoners off?

Those abolitionists who see LWOP as an acceptable alternative to execution do not realize that in essence they are supporting a penalty that is more cruel and harder on the individual than is outright execution. We should not be deceived into wasting our valuable time, efforts and resources by validating a punishment that is worse than death, that prolongs the suffering for the rest of a prisoner's existence, a future in which there is no hope. We need to focus on the eradication of capital punishment, but not to allow society to clean it up by giving more LWOP sentences as an alternative.

Don't give me life without hope, for we all have humanity and dignity and should not be discarded as if we were human waste. Many people have asked me if I was given the choice to decide if I would accept a resentencing that would change my death sentence into LWOP would I accept it? I do not have to think about it in order to answer. The answer is no.

Chapter 5

The Execution Protocol

When the condemned is served with an execution warrant, a packet of documents is provided which must be filled out. The actual "execution protocol," the policy that lists the step-by-step procedure and timetable for an execution, will be revealed in its entirety. Usually we death row prisoners are never allowed to see the actual policy. It is considered a security issue. So they can kill us, but we are not to know the procedure. That is ridiculous.

However, in April of 1998, I filed a "Petition for Post Conviction Relief," pro se, in the Superior Court of Maricopa County, Arizona (see Appendix, page 175). One of the issues that I presented was the issue of cruel and unusual punishment of execution by lethal injection. Thus I was able to obtain a copy of the execution protocol under the discovery process so that I could include it in the petition. This was before we were moved to SMU II, and some of the procedures have changed in a minor way. Those changes only have to do with logistics, such as the time of day which was moved to 3p.m. from midnight. We are still blindly led like sheep to slaughter. I used to believe that keeping the execution protocol a secret was because the department was ashamed of what they were doing. After watching 22 men executed, I do not believe there is any shame on their part. They are an efficient killing machine.

It is fitting that this book draws to a close with the execution protocol. Just as the death row prisoner's life ends in real life. It is quite an elaborate and well thought out production that could rival a successful Broadway play, only it plays to a very select audience behind thick walls and locked doors. A tremendous amount of effort goes into all the details for our final curtain call.

Over the years, I have observed that there are four elements necessary for carrying out executions:

1. Demonize the killer.
2. Authorize executions.
3. Automate executions.
4. Ritualize executions.

We demonize the killer in the eye of society as an individual of no worth and value. The killer is portrayed as a cancer on society that must be exorcised at all costs. Then we authorize executions by brainwashing the public into believing the lie that the only way to deter crime and prevent future murders is to make an example out of killers by executing them. This just perpetuates the cycle of violence and educates our children that killing is okay, that we can kill as punishment. They also claim that once the killer is dead, he certainly cannot kill again. A life sentence in prison would prevent him from killing again, but that is not good enough. We then automate the flow of executions through the passing of laws in Congress and the individual states with the stamp of approval from the US Supreme Court. When we feel that executions are not moving along fast enough, new laws are enacted, like the Antiterrorism and Effective Death Penalty Act (AEDPA). That law added 60 new crimes that can be punished with the death penalty and imposed severe limitations on the Habeas Corpus Petition that all the condemned prisoners file in the Federal District courts. A convict has one year to file in the federal court after having completed the state court appeals. If it is not filed in that time, they are out of luck. The petition must be completed within 180 days, and then the judge is bound to rule on the petition within 120 days. The rule is hard and fast. A second or successive habeas petition cannot be filed without first gaining the approval of a three-judge panel in the Court of Appeals for that district court.

That system cuts off years of appeals. Furthermore, the federal judges are restricted as to what issues they can review in a petition from the state courts. Previously, if you could prove that the state court judges had incorrectly or wrongly interpreted the law, the federal judge was obligated to overturn the verdict. With the AEDPA, the federal judges can only intervene in cases when the state court decision is "contrary, or involved an unreasonable application of clearly established federal law." Plainly speaking, this means the state court judges can incorrectly interpret the law, as long as it is not done in an unreasonable way. And if you do not bring or develop an issue in the state court first, you cannot raise it for the first time in the federal court.

Lastly, we ritualize the executions through such procedures as the execution protocol. We have not evolved much from ancient civilizations that ritualized their killings and offerings to their gods. We have just updated the procedure. We offer up these killings to those who have been victimized as well as to the huge voting constituency that hungers for the violence, retribution and blood vengeance. The public should not be fooled into thinking it is for any other purpose. There is an old saying, "To the victor goes the spoils!" In this case, the victor is the politician who campaigns and is elected on the "get tough on crime" rhetoric and the pro-death penalty platform. And the spoils are the executions put on for the population that clamors for its legally begotten ration of death and gore. Just as the Romans threw their slaves and criminals into the lion's pit to appease the crowds, someone must be made to pay for the ills of society.

Some information concerning the execution and the procedures of how an execution is carried out are made available to the public on ADOC's website. There is a complete index of all the death row prisoners and their prison numbers. Each prisoner has a page that profiles the crime and other relevant information. After that, there is a section containing historical information back to the days when people were hung in Arizona. The death house has its own section. A picture can be found of the gas chamber and the lethal injection gurney. The procedures and a list of the chemicals (poisons) that are used to execute a person are clearly identified. All this is made clear for public consumption. We, the death row prisoners, are not aware of this. All we have to do is to wait. Just before an execution, members of the public can obtain the date and time of the event, any last minute stays of execution and the condemned person's last meal list.

THE DOCUMENTS OF DEATH

The correctional service counselor or the supervisor will serve a copy of the execution warrant along with a packet of forms that are to be filled out by the condemned prisoner in order to facilitate the execution. These include:

1. The Warrant of Execution. An actual execution warrant is presented at the back of this book so that you can read the words that are used in order to legally kill a person [see Appendix, p209].
2. Notificaton Letter. Upon issuance of an execution warrant, the Board of Executive Clemency will notify the prisoner that a date has been set for a Clemency Hearing [see Appendix, p211].
3. Clemency Attendance Form. The prisoner is asked to check off whether he will or will not attend the Clemency Hearing [see Appendix, p212].
4. Clemency Board Form—Clemency Request. That is a so-called, "Plea for Relief" [see Appendix, p214].

When I received my execution warrant in 1996, I refused my right to a clemency hearing. Since no death row prisoner in Arizona has ever been granted clemency, what is the purpose of the charade? Most men do attend their hearings and beg for their lives. What happens is that the prisoner is hauled over to a hearing room where they are restrained and locked into a little cage on display for all to see. Reporters and photographers are there along with the victim's family, the prosecution, the defense attorney and witnesses.

The state reviews the case and crime in an abridged manner and makes sure to point out what a monster the condemned is and that they do not deserve any mercy. Then the victim's family has their chance to describe all the pain and suffering that has been caused for them. That is all designed to portray to the Clemency Board that the convict should not be spared. The attorney then sets out to undo all the negative statements made against the condemned through his own statements and witnesses. Regretfully, that always come up short. It is just another opportunity to humiliate and demonize the prisoner in the public's eye. It is a farce. The members of the Clemency Board are appointed by the governor and they know where their alliance lies. Death row clemency is never granted. All of the 22 executions since 1992 have gone on as scheduled. The hearings are put on to give the appearance of legitimacy. There is no purpose to being dragged before the cameras one last time to convince the public that it is right to kill.

I agree that victims have their rights. They have suffered terrible losses. Each of them deals with their loss in a number of ways. Some forgive. Some put it behind them and go on with their lives. Others are blinded by the rhetoric of "closure" and prefer blood vengeance. The condemned have only one reality to deal with. They are punished relentlessly from the very first day on the row until the execution. It is a continual grinding down process that goes on. The most hardened of killers cannot deny what they have done that has put them where they are. There are no distractions from the punishment. To many on the row, death is welcomed as an end to this perpetual nightmare. We actually suffer for so many years waiting to be executed, that we serve a life sentence before being executed.

Therefore, why would any death row prisoner want to be paraded before the public at a clemency hearing at the end of his/her life, to permit yet another assault on what remains of their dignity? I think not.

Most people do not think that the condemned suffer sufficiently. I hope you will know by now that we agonize daily. That is not to say we don't deserve punishment for our misdeeds. But in today's revenge-driven environment, too many people are convinced that life is too easy on death row and that we do not pay harshly enough for our crimes. I cannot argue that some crimes are just so horrific that they are in a class by themselves. However, many of the murderers on death row are here because they have committed felony murder but not those terrible, unspeakable acts against mankind. They are not heinous or deviant murderers. When a murder is committed in the process of a robbery, that qualifies for the death penalty. Those are not remarkable crimes and certainly not the worst of the worst. Society is entitled to its punishment and revenge, but all too often, we are paying more than we were sentenced to pay, and that is criminal in itself.

CLEMENCY REQUEST—PLEA FOR RELIEF

If a prisoner plans to attend their clemency hearing, they must fill out a form. They must state what they wish the Board of

Pardons and Paroles to recommend to the Governor. They are asked to rate their behavior while incarcerated, what positive accomplishments they have made (such as educational and vocational programs), why they believe they are entitled to a sentence change, to admit their involvement in the crime they were sentenced for, what their plans would be if they were released, and any other relevant information.

When a prisoner is on death row their conduct does not matter whatsoever in the Board's decision. Positive programming and rehabilitation count for zero as well. After all, they were deemed not rehabilitatable due to the fact that they were sentenced to die. It is ridiculous to ask these questions of a death row prisoner. The Board knows why they are on death row—that is to die. No one can undo their crime by being a model prisoner!

I have seen men who genuinely changed for the better go to the clemency hearing—men who were supported by their judge, the prosecution, the FBI and the victim's family members, all asking that the board spare this person, only to be denied. The Board is just not willing to give a person a second chance at life.

When the executions resumed here in 1992 and Donald Harding died a gruesome and painful execution in the gas chamber, the legislature passed a new law making lethal injection the method of execution for those sentenced after 1992. Those convicted before 1992 could choose gas or lethal injection. Since the Ninth Circuit Court of Appeals had ruled the gas chamber to be cruel and unusual punishment, for years Arizona death row prisoners tried to halt their executions by choosing cyanide gas to get a stay in the Ninth Circuit. All have failed.

Such was the case with Karl and Walter LaGrand, two German citizens executed in Arizona. I knew them both from the first day I came to death row. They both attended their clemency hearings. They both elected to die as they were sentenced, by the gas chamber. By choosing gas as his method of execution, Karl knew that the Ninth Circuit Court of Appeals would issue a stay of execution. Once the stay was granted, the state appealed to the US Supreme Court in order to get the stay lifted. The Supreme Court, our guardians of morality and law, quickly lifted the stay. The execution would proceed. Uncharacteristically, the state then allowed Karl to change from cyanide gas to lethal injection. At a certain point, the condemned cannot change execution methods. It was not so much that the state was being kind, rather that they clearly understood the negative implications of gassing a German citizen with the German government's representatives watching; it harked one back to the days of the Holocaust when millions were gassed to death. How embarrassing and ironic to gas a German citizen. When all of the last minute "gang plank" appeals failed, the poison flowed into Karl's veins putting him into the big sleep.

Just seven days later, his brother Walter was scheduled to be executed by cyanide gas. During Walter's clemency hearing he apologized numerous times to all the victims' families. The German government raised the issue that the LaGrand brothers were not allowed to contact their German consular officials when they were arrested. The issue was also brought to the International Court of Justice in The Hague, Netherlands. Also, at the clemency hearing, the state admitted that they knew the brothers were German and should have been allowed to make the phone call. The denial of the phone call violated International Treaties. In an unexpected move, the clemency board voted 2–1 to recommend to Governor Jane Hull that a 60-day stay of execution be allowed so that this issue could be properly addressed. This was the first time the clemency board recommended anything less than death. However, Governor Hull was quick to deny this request and proceed with the execution. The dilemma Hull faced was that if she allowed the 60-day stay and at some point relief was granted to Walter and he could not be executed, then how does she deal with having killed Karl LaGrand the week before? So she had to see to it that Walter's execution proceeded. The loose ends had to be tidied up. Politics as usual.

So Walter entered the gas chamber. He was executed at 9:30 p.m. It was a painful death. Can you imagine watching as a man goes into spasms and endless involuntary convulsions for 18 minutes? What kind of society does this to its citizens? It belies the wisdom of the US Supreme Court to allow executions in the gas chamber. After all, they have said cyanide gas was not "cruel and unusual." None of the Supreme Court justices have actually experienced being strapped inside of a gas chamber and made to suck in cyanide vapors to test their beliefs. They say that justice is blind for a reason.

Again, it seems our society has not learned from history. For the past 50 years the world has condemned gassing human beings. Does the Holocaust and the "final solution" mean anything? We must have forgotten that lesson. The German people have struggled all these years to overcome the evils of their past mistakes. How cruel and hypocritical then not to stop the death of two of their own in a gas chamber. How insensitive.

Why does the world community allow this? We put people to death with cyanide gas in private. We only allow the victim's family, prisoner's family and a few reporters to watch the event. No matter how many times witnesses relate the horrors of these spectacles, the executions continue. The executions are not even newsworthy any more and rarely get mentioned. Walter could have changed the method from gas to lethal injection, but he chose to take gas in the hope that some public consciousness would be raised. The jury is still out on that. Take care, Walter. I'll see you in another lifetime, hopefully a lifetime with more compassion and a lot less pain and suffering.

A little-known fact is that when someone is executed, the body loses control of its functions and the person will defecate and urinate on themselves. One of the procedures before an execution is to have the condemned put on an adult diaper so that the staff does not have to clean up the mess. Before the advent of adult diapers, the proverbial "butt plug" was rumored to be used. However, nothing can be done to conceal the drooling, vomiting, violent muscle spasms and contractions, swelling of the skin tissue and the odor of burning flesh.

Lethal injection is not a new idea. It has been around a long time. Looking back to 1939, the Nazi government encouraged doctors to become direct participants in state-sponsored killings. The national euthanasia program was developed and put into use in 1939 for the purpose of disposing of large numbers of physically and mentally handicapped patients. State sponsored killing was a key feature of the Third Reich. The killings were ideologically motivated to enhance the image of the so-called "master race."

In the 1970s, during the moratorium on executions by the US Supreme Court, Oklahoma's electric chair had deteriorated so badly that is was going to cost $60,000 to repair it. The state did not want to invest that much money in the chair so they consulted the department of Anesthesiology at the University of Oklahoma in an attempt to find a cheaper method of execution. Professor Stanley Deutsch came up with the idea of using a barbiturate to kill the pain, followed by a muscle relaxant to stop breathing. It was an ideal and inexpensive method to bring about a speedy death. That became the law in Oklahoma in 1978, but it was Texas that first used it in 1982. By 1999, 95 percent of all executions were by lethal injection.

Physicians' participation in executions is specifically condemned by the American Medical Association. The AMA's Council on Ethical and Judicial Affairs states that a physician "should not be a participant in a legally authorized execution." The AMA outlines eight specific banned practices that constitute direct participation in an execution, including injecting lethal drugs, selecting IV sites, monitoring vital signs and pronouncing death.

In 2001, it became a crime in Tennessee to use pancuronium bromide in the euthanasia of animals, but it is still allowed in 31 states for the lethal injection of humans. pancuronium bromide paralyzes the skeletal muscles but does not affect the brain or nervous system. A person injected with it remains conscious and can feel pain but cannot speak.

In court testimony against the use of pancuronium bromide, Carol Weihrer stated that she had undergone eye surgery in 1998 when pancuronium bromide was used in order to immobilize the eye. But the anesthetic was ineffective. She testified that the experience was terrifying and tortuous. She could not communicate that she was awake and in great pain. She tried to use all of her strength to move and signal but with no success. She was on a respirator for breathing. The surgery lasted over an hour. She called the experience, "worse than death."

The trade name for pancuronium bromide is, "Pavulon." Recently a judge, Ellen Hobbs Lyle, stated that Pavulon had no legitimate purpose. The subject gives the appearance of a serene reaction when in reality they are feeling the excruciating painful ordeal of death by lethal injection. Pavulon gives the false impression of calmness to viewers, making punishment by lethal injection palatable and acceptable to society. However, despite the judge's misgivings she ruled that the use of the drug in executions did not violate the constitutional ban on cruel and unusual punishment, because it is widely used and because there is less than a remote chance that the prisoner will be subjected to unnecessary pain or suffering.

It is ironic that the American Veterinary Association condemns the use of pancuronium bromide in animals whether used by itself or in combination with sodium phenobarbital. They stated that "the animal may perceive pain and distress after it has been immobilized." The state uses the logic that the ban on pancuronium bromide to euthanize pets does not apply to human prisoners because they are not non-livestock animals, which the law says includes pets, captured wildlife, domesticated animals, rabbits, ducks and pigs. So, convicted prisoners are to be considered as less than animals.

When lethal injection is used, another form of torture can result. Since many condemned prisoners are intravenous drug users, their veins are almost impossible to locate to insert the intravenous line. As a result, a cut down procedure must be done. A scalpel is used (without anesthesia) to cut open the arm or leg to find the vein. Then there are blowouts. That is when the tube blows out of the arm when the fatal cocktail is pumped through the line. All of these actions cause severe pain to the individual. But the public still believes that lethal injection is a peaceful and painless method of death. As peaceful as putting an unwanted pet to sleep. A perfect example of this occurred just recently in Florida. The following is from an article in the *New York Times*, dated June 9, 2000:

> KILLER'S FINAL WORDS REVEAL TROUBLE WITH LETHAL INJECTION
>
> Miami, Florida, which switched to lethal injection after a series of botched executions in the electric chair, has had trouble with another execution.
>
> Bennie Demps, a three-time convicted killer sentenced to die by lethal injection on Wednesday, was strapped to a gurney for 33 minutes while, he said, in his final words, technicians at Florida State Prison struggled to insert the lethal intravenous drip in his veins. When the procedure to insert the intravenous drip, which

normally takes a few minutes, was completed and the curtain between the execution chamber and witnesses was opened, Demps pleaded with his lawyer to investigate the way the state's executioners handled him.

"They butchered me back there," Demps said. "I was in a lot of pain. They cut me in the groin, they cut me in the leg. I was bleeding profusely. This is not an execution, it is murder."

The state went ahead with the execution, its third since shifting from the electric chair in February.

A Spokesman for Gov. Jeb Bush said Demps was strapped to the gurney for so long because the paperwork was delayed, and because the technicians had trouble finding a vein.

Demps' lawyer, George F. Shaefer, told the *Miami Herald* that the court had notified the warden by 5:30 p.m. that it would not act on the case. Demps, his lawyer said in a written statement, was pronounced dead at 6:53 p.m.

Here in Arizona the ADOC goes out of its way to obfuscate and conceal from the public when problems occur with executions. On February 16, 2000, Anthony Chaney was executed by lethal injection. No mention was ever released to the press or the public that a problem had occurred.

It was only due to the fact that the Federal Public Defender's Office hired a pathologist to be present at the autopsy of Anthony Chaney that it became known that in order to execute Chaney, a cut down was crudely done with a scalpel on both of his legs in order to insert the intravenous lines to enable the poison to flow into his body and kill him. The pain and suffering involved in this cut down has still not been acknowledged by the ADOC. When the curtains were opened for the witnesses at the execution, the condemned was already strapped on the gurney and covered with a sheet. No one could see the cut down that was performed underneath. Out of sight, out of mind. Should anyone still think that execution by lethal injection is painless, think again.

So it is not just the electric chair that malfunctions during executions: even the so-called humane lethal injection is not foolproof. This type of event happens more often than the public is made aware of. In their zeal to put on their little "dog and pony show" for the public, it matters little how much pain may be inflicted on the condemned. After all, who cares; the condemned is dead meat one way or the other. If cutting someone open twice, causing them to bleed profusely, then being stitched up raw, only to be then strapped on the execution gurney, with outstretched arms, eyes focused on the ceiling waiting for 33 minutes until hearing the plungers click that indicate death is coming, is not the most blatant torture, I don't know what is.

When most people see death approaching, it is described as the most excruciating fear imaginable. A few seconds of such anticipation has been known to kill someone. Imagine being made to wait 33 minutes for your deliverance. What is wrong with this picture?

BODY SNATCHERS

One morning we were awakened by the sound of inmates being moved. All ten prisoners in pod number 2 were being moved. Before we knew it, all ten were gone and the pod was completely empty. A few mornings later, heavy construction was going on. Sparks were flying, drills were whining and hammers were banging. The racket went on for several days. No one could figure out what was happening. Curiosity can drive you mad around here. It was not until 14 days before a scheduled execution that we figured out what was taking place. They moved the condemned man into the empty pod number two, which was now going to be used as the death watch cell, instead of transporting the prisoner back to CB6. Video cameras and VCR where installed in the guard tower. Now every move could be observed and simultaneously recorded on videotape for 24 hours a day.

We cannot just ignore such activities aimed at hastening or facilitating our execution. It is just another form of torture in disguise. Some tortures are subtle while others are done so flagrantly that no one can miss the message or intent.

When in the observation cell we have nothing. Each morning we are given an orange jumpsuit and bed linens are collected. The cell is searched and we begin the day. In the evening, we surrender our jumpsuit and are given new bed linen. All this done so that we do not hang ourselves. We are allowed one sheet of paper to write on and a three-inch pencil stub. To get another sheet of paper we must surrender the first sheet of paper. It is futile to try to make sense out of these rituals. Needless to say, it is difficult to write farewell letters under such circumstances.

In those last two weeks before an execution the only visitors allowed are our immediate family, attorneys, and clergy. Our friends who are on the approved visitation list are not allowed to visit, even though this is the time they would most like to be with us and we would most like to see them. If there is no immediate family, then we get no visits. As far as phone calls are concerned, we can only have the regular weekly phone call to someone on our visitation/phone list. No extra calls. We can speak to our attorney as often as possible. This is a cold and calculated policy. All we are told is what follows:

1. Condemned Inmate Witness List. The condemned prisoner can request five witnesses to be invited to view the execution and can also request a clergy member to be present. [See Appendix, page 222.]
2. Disposition of Property. The condemned prisoner must designate an individual to whom your personal property is to be released to. If they do not, the property will be donated to the state. [See Appendix, page 223.]
3. Disposition of Remains. The condemned prisoner is asked to give the name of a surviving spouse who will be responsible for the funeral and burial arrangements. If there is no spouse, or if the spouse is not financially able to provide for burial, they turn to the adult children. If the condemned prisoner has no adult children or they cannot afford to provide for the burial, the body will be released to ADOC and will be buried in the county "Potters Field" or the cemetery located in Florence, Arizona. No names are placed on the graves, only a number. The public is not permitted to visit these gravesites. [See Appendix, page 224.]

4. Last Will and Testament. A standard will form is provided so that the condemned prisoner can designate an executor for their estate. [See Appendix, page 226.]
5. Last Meal Request. The condemned is given the opportunity to choose a last meal. There are restrictions. The items requested must be available in the prison food inventory or able to be purchased locally in a grocery store. The quantity of food is determined by what can be consumed in a half hour. [See Appendix, page 227.]

No one is sure of the roots of the last meal tradition. It has been researched back to 15th-century England. It is said that the wardens and sheriffs did not want the condemned going to their death thinking bad of them, so they offered them food and drink. I have read that there are individuals in society who maintain computer files on all the death row prisoners nationwide. Of particular interest to them is the food selection for the last meal. This begs a question, do we like the prisoner who only orders a hamburger better than the prisoner who orders steak and eggs for the last meal? Even to the bitter end, the condemned is judged.

DEATH WATCH

The death-watch experience arouses anxiety. When a prisoner is separated from his pod, he loses the ability to use any human powers. There is no activity; he is helpless, apart from the world as he knows it. He is vulnerable to attacks and cannot react. Intense anxiety increasingly develops, as well as feelings of shame and guilt. He is naked to himself. He only wants to leave this prison of loneliness. It is easy to go insane.

That is why so many of the condemned seem incoherent and have dazed expressions on their faces. It is all part of the experience, and torture, of the execution protocol. The ritual of pain. The mental agony does not start there, at the end; it starts the first day we arrive on death row, although we do not realize it at the time. We are reduced to the smallest common denominator. We have just the clothes on our back. The pain and loneliness creeps up slowly and eventually overcomes us. Many do not see it coming and never realize how they have been changed in the process of dehumanization. The gradual process makes you feel inadequate and worthless. For years we are told we have no value and are treated as though we have no human qualities, and eventually we come to accept it. It is akin to the invasion of the body snatchers.

Until you are put into such a situation, you can never understand what it means to be looking over your shoulder, as in my case for 20 years, wondering when your time is up. Our minds may run from it, but we can never escape the inevitability. It is a closed course with no exit doors. Periodic detours with false hope are thrown into the mix only to add more pain and disillusionment. We are allowed to suffer the desperation of dashed hopes as part of the punishment. When this happens over and over again, we become desensitized to the process. I would not leave my cell to go back to court if I had an evidentiary hearing on any legal matter to resolve. I would just let my attorney go. After all, it is the attorney, not me, who the judge listens to. It is too painful to be put through the rollercoaster of pain that results from being denied relief. Twice I went back to court to be resentenced, convinced by my attorney that I would not get the death sentence again, only to be given it again, each time. It is an emotional disaster. If we are to survive for years in this environment, we must harden ourselves against the game of indulgent pain and suffering. If we succumb to all of this, our death comes much sooner than our actual execution.

THE PROTOCOL

It is a cold-blooded and morbid to have to walk, step by step, from a cell to a grave, from life to death. Here is the lethal injection procedure. To the best of my knowledge, the following procedures will take place to cause my death by lethal injection:

- At approximately 2:30 p.m. on the day prior to the scheduled execution, the Special Operations Team Leader and designated medical staff member will conduct an inventory of equipment and materials.
- At approximately 4:00 p.m. on the day prior to the scheduled execution, all inventoried materials, equipment, and drugs, will be secured in the equipment area adjacent to the execution chamber.
- At approximately 9:00 p.m. on the day prior to the scheduled execution, the executioners will arrive at Arizona State Prison, Florence.
- At approximately 9:05 p.m. on the day prior to the scheduled execution, the drug box will be delivered to the warden.
- At approximately 9:10 p.m. on the day prior to the scheduled execution, the warden will deliver the drug box to the executioners.
- At approximately 10:00 p.m. on the day prior to the scheduled execution, the Special Operations Team Restraint Team

will report to the Special Operations Team Leader in the execution building security area. At about the same time either the Director of ADOC or the warden will place a telephone call to the Governor of Arizona.

- At approximately 10:05 p.m. on the day prior to the scheduled execution, a medical doctor will arrive at the Arizona State Prison, Florence.
- At approximately 10:30 p.m. on the day prior to the scheduled execution, a final briefing will be held with the Special Operations Restraint Team by the Special Operations Team Leader.
- At approximately 11:00 p.m. on the day prior to the scheduled execution, the warden will give the signal to proceed.
- At approximately 11:05 p.m. on the day prior to the scheduled execution, the Special Operations Team Restraint Team will remove me from my cell, conduct a strip search, and escort me to the execution chamber. At that time the Director of ADOC will ask me if I have any last words.
- At approximately 11:30 p.m. on the day prior to the scheduled execution, the restraint of me will be completed and the Special Operations Team will exit the execution chamber.
- Between 11:35 and 11:55 p.m. on the day prior to the scheduled execution, the executioners will insert the IVs into my arms and a heart monitor will be positioned on my chest.
- At approximately 11:55 p.m. on the day prior to the scheduled execution, the witnesses to the execution will be admitted to the witness observation area.
- At approximately 12:02 a.m. on the day of the scheduled

execution, a medical examiner will be admitted to the staging area and the warden will give a signal that the witnesses are in place.

- At approximately 12:03 a.m. on the day of the scheduled execution, the Director of ADOC may tell the witnesses that there has been no reprieve.
- At approximately 12:04 a.m. on the day of the scheduled execution, the Director of ADOC tells the warden to proceed and the Special Operations Team Leader will exit the execution chamber. After a 30 second wait, the blinds to the witness area will be opened.
- At approximately 12:05 a.m. on the day of the scheduled execution, the warden will tell the executioners to proceed and the execution will commence.
- At approximately 12:10 a.m. on the day of the execution, the executioners will notify the warden when the execution is completed. The warden will await a signal from the medical doctor that the heart monitor indicates death.
- At approximately 12:20 a.m. on the day of the execution, the blinds to the witness area will be closed. The medical examiner will be admitted to the execution chamber.
- At approximately 12:25 a.m. on the day of the execution, either the Director of ADOC or the warden will advise the witnesses that the execution was completed.

THE DRUGS

The following drugs will be used to cause death: sodium pentothal, pancuronium (Pavulon) and potassium chloride. In addition, Valium, lidocaine HCL (Xylocaine), epinephrine,

Narcan, morphine and Demorol are available for use during the lethal injection process. Of these drugs, sodium pentothal, Valium, Narcan, morphine, and Demerol are all medications which are controlled substances under federal drug regulations and are approved only for medicinal use, not for executions. Possession and use of these drugs is restricted to individuals properly licensed by the Food and Drug Administration.

Sodium pentothal, pancuronium and potassium chloride are prescription drugs as defined by Arizona Revised Statute 32-1901 (57)a, which provides: "[a]ny drug which because of its toxicity or other potentiality for harmful effect, or the method of its use, or the collateral measures necessary to its use, is not generally recognized among experts … as safe for use except by or under the supervision of a medical practitioner." The "prescription only drugs" that will be used to cause my death will not be used for the intended therapeutic value.

Chapter 6

Recent Challenges to the Death Penalty Offer Hope

You can compare a sentence of death to a fatal disease. When someone is told they have a fatal disease, they inevitably ask when they will die. Some diseases are merciful. They destroy the person quickly. Others are very debilitating, and take much longer. Scientists struggle to find the cures. Money is no object. After all, many diseases kill, and since we abhor death and love life, we want most of all to prevent death. We try to find vaccines that can be used to immunize society from life-threatening diseases. Some deaths are difficult to prevent. We hate the years of suffering that often accompany the process of dying. Such suffering seems unfair. We regret that we cannot stop this senseless dying, but it is not man-made. It is out of our control. We fight with passion, and a love for life. But there is another death, another cancer, a man-made one. We call it capital punishment. It is crueler than any disease. This death is the most excruciating of all. The individual under this particular sentence of death is made to suffer for what seems like endless lifetimes.

The waiting, the loneliness, the false hopes, the delays, the humiliation, the futility, the desperation, and the loss of dignity, freedom and choice combine to create the most agonizingly stressful and painful existence one can imagine or endure. There are no painkillers that can be given.

The sadness concerning this disease is that a cure exists. It does not require legions of scientists to find the solution, it is known. It has been known for an eternity. All that it would take is a mixture of common sense, love, some conscience, humility and compassion, simply to realize that we can put a stop to this plague by just by saying no. No more draining of the human spirit, punishing individuals by allowing them to sit and slowly die for as long as 20 years on death row.

We cringe when we learn about animals being used for scientific research. We deplore any unnecessary pain to which such animals are subjected in laboratory experiments, usually resulting in death. We cry out that these practices be halted. But what is a man? Is he not as important as an animal? If society could know the suffering involved in this uniquely slow death on death row, then they might yell out loud enough for others to hear. We might then urge the use of the cure that just requires saying no. No more madness. When will we put an end to this quest for revenge?

"When will we put an end to this quest for revenge?" I doubt I will see an answer to this question in what is left of my lifetime. But it is encouraging to see the moratorium movement picking up support. To see Governor Ryan in Illinois declare a moratorium in January 2003 was tremendous. Other states have passed legislation to install moratoriums, only to be vetoed by their governors. Then there is the movement toward a federal moratorium, and we thought that president Clinton would postpone those upcoming federal executions, but he did not. It had been a long time since the federal government executed anyone. They did not even have a federal death house until recently. It seemed like it was only a matter of time before a nationwide moratorium was put into place. It may take longer than we think, but I feel it will occur.

Governor Ryan's decision to pardon four death row prisoners and commute the remaining 167 death sentences, to life without parole, is perhaps the single most important development in the recent history of the abolition movement.

History has a way of surprising us. After all, who would have thought that the Republican Governor of Illinois would be anything more than just one more "tough on crime" conservative? Paradoxically, Ryan emerged as a liberal republican. Webster's Dictionary defines liberalism as "a political philosophy based upon a belief in progress, the essential goodness of man, and the autonomy of the individual and standing up for the protection of political and civil liberties." Certainly, this is what George Ryan has done. He stood up for these principles when few others would. This is a man who has acted on his convictions and conscience, a man of great courage. I personally rank him up there with the likes of Abe Lincoln, Lyndon Johnson, Martin Luther King Jr. and Nelson Mandela, who have all advanced the cause of civil liberties and civil rights.

Our history will tell what lasting effect Ryan's actions will have on the quest to abolish capital punishment in America. Some victims and their families decry this act as a betrayal in its highest form. They object to all of those who are now getting life sentences because they are convinced that these prisoners are guilty of murder and are now escaping a just punishment. One cannot dispute that many are guilty, but as recent history has shown, well over 100 death row prisoners have been set free because they were found to be innocent. Ryan studied the problem and the recommendations of a blue ribbon commission composed of some of the brightest and most experienced legal minds in Illinois. He realized that there was plenty of guilt on death row, but he also recognized that many did not get a fair shake from the legal system. There was also poverty, racism and a corrupt judicial system. All those beatings, confessions, and poor lawyering contributing to the arbitrary and capricious, yet deliberate, assignment of death as a penalty in Illinois.

He also took note of the fact that there had been 33 lawyers who were disbarred or suspended during this period. Of the 85 specific recommendations to correct the death penalty in Illinois, none were approved by the state legislature. In the end, Ryan saw mass commutation as the only solution when his time in office ran out. No matter what he did, one side would be angry. And for a republican politician to make such an act against all odds, in my opinion, is one of the most courageous acts in a lifetime.

Abolitionists should not be lulled into becoming lax in their actions to oppose capital punishment. Although disparaged by Ryan's action, prosecutors in Illinois loudly state that they will continue to prosecute as they always have. One stated, "I will not let one moment in time, which I do not believe was well reasoned and well thought out, to change a process and system that has worked." What an amazing statement! I hope prospective jurors will take notice of the mass commutations and pardons and this will cause them difficulties in believing that the death penalty is a just, fair and reasonable option. It cannot be gauged at this time whether this momentous action taken by Ryan will have any effect on the remaining 37 states and the federal government who apply the death penalty. This could, after all, be just an aberration.

There are strong conservative forces that resist change. Conservative judges are people who hold primitive views on a host of momentous questions such as the death penalty, affirmative action, privacy and abortion. One only has to look at a recent statement by Supreme Court Justice Clarence Thomas. A death row prisoner in Florida submitted a writ of certiorari to the Supreme Court, claiming it was "cruel and unusual" punishment that he has been made to suffer the tortures of death row for 28 years. Most cert writs are denied without comment, however, this time Clarence Thomas chose to issue a scathing response. He admonished the prisoner by telling him it would not have been cruel and unusual punishment if he, the prisoner, would have simply submitted to the will of the state of Florida years ago and just taken his punishment of execution. How does one counter such a statement? This is the face of conservatism in America today.

Abolition is a long and hard road with few victories. Therefore, such extraordinary action as Governor Ryan has done will serve to rejuvenate and fuel us on in the struggle. Tremendously wonderful things can come from totally unexpected quarters. Everyone is capable of teaching us the lesson of understanding, fairness and the desire to do the right thing under the harshest circumstances and pressure. Governor Ryan has displayed the mettle that greatness comes from. We are all in his debt.

* * *

Some other major developments concerning the death penalty, that affect death row prisoners in Arizona, Idaho, Montana, and to a lesser degree, in Nebraska and Colorado, are still ongoing.

An Arizona death row prisoner, Timothy Ring, raised an issue in his appeal that was based upon a previous New Jersey case, entitled Apprendi v. New Jersey 530 US 466 (2000). The Apprendi case is not a death penalty case. Apprendi had been found guilty of firing a weapon at a home where a black family lived. At the time of his sentencing the judge made the determination that the crime qualified as a hate crime. As such, he was sentenced to an enhanced term of years, more than he would otherwise have been subject to. The judge created the aggravating circumstance of a hate crime without that factor having been determined by the jury. The judge decided on the aggravating factor that increased the penalty, on his own. The US Supreme Court held that the aggravating factor which enhanced the sentence must be determined by a jury.

In June 2002, Timothy Ring successfully challenged the Arizona death penalty sentencing procedure by claiming that it violated the Sixth Amendment guarantee of a trial by a jury of one's peers, as affirmed in Apprendi. Arizona's death penalty law, which placed the death penalty decision solely upon the judge, had been upheld by the US Supreme Court in Walton v. Arizona 497 US 637 (1990). The Supreme Court now declared in Ring that they had erred in Walton and overturned the Arizona death penalty law because it allowed a judge without a jury to find an aggravating circumstance necessary for imposition of the death penalty. Now, any such aggravating factor must be determined by the jury rather than a judge if a death penalty is to be imposed.

The US Supreme Court decided Ring v. Arizona No. 01-488, in Ring's favor, by a 7 to 2 vote, with the two dissenting votes cast by Chief Justice Rehnquist and Sandra Day O'Connor, both of whom are from Arizona. Since the old law was declared unconstitutional, no one could then be sentenced until a new law was written, so the Arizona state legislature called a special session to rewrite the sentencing laws to comply with Ring. The then state Attorney General, Janet Napolitano, who had unsuccessfully argued in the Supreme Court against Ring, was in the midst of running a campaign for governorship when the Ring decision came down. She then came forward, in an effort at damage control and political spin, to declare that the Ring decision would only apply to 30 of the 127 death penalty prisoners in Arizona. Those 30 were still in the early stages of their appeals in state courts, but she did not envision that Ring would apply retroactively to the other 97 who were in federal court with their appeals.

Some legal experts argued that changing a judicial system that is centered around judges to a system centered around juries is a complex change and should not be rushed into. There are ex-post facto elements that forbid prisoners from being resentenced under a new statute that did not exist at the time they committed their offense. Many people called for a moratorium until there could be a review of the entire capital punishment process, but that effort fell on deaf ears in Arizona.

On June 26, 2002, National Public Radio interviewed me on the air, covering the recent developments in the Ring case.

It was heard across the country and went as follows:

> Profile: Death row inmate, Richard Rossi, and what impact a Supreme Court decision overturning some death sentences might have on his case.
>
> Bob Edwards, host: This week the US Supreme Court overturned the death sentences of many convicted murderers because judges, not juries, decided their punishment. The Supreme Court ruling arose from a case known as Ring v. Arizona. Arizona's death row inmates are celebrating. Still, some wonder if the ruling will help them. NPR's Wendy Kaufman has one man's story.
>
> Wendy Kaufman, reporting: Richard Rossi has been on Arizona's death row for 19 years, locked in a cinder block room 23 hours a day with almost no human contact. He can yell down the hall to other inmates, and for the past several months Rossi and a couple of others in his unit have been talking about the case before the Supreme Court. Because everyone can hear everyone else's conversations, most of the men in nearby cells knew about the case and its potential impact. Rossi heard about the decision on the radio, and within a few minutes he had spread the word to the nine other men in his pod.
>
> Richard Rossi (death row inmate): About an hour later when the rest of the population started to hear the news on radio and TV, there was little bits of screams and yells up and down. "Hey, Joe, did you hear the death penalty was overturned?" or, you know, "Mike, did you hear this?" And it was heartwarming that these guys have some hope, you know, because there is very little hope in here.

Kaufman: Rossi is not a typical death row inmate. He's a college graduate, and worked as an accountant. But like so many others involved in violent crime, Rossi started using drugs. His wife left him, and things fell apart. Later, he managed to kick his cocaine habit, and he moved to Arizona.

Rossi: I was doing pretty well, and then another personal situation came up and I wound up reverting back to some drugs, and I committed a crime under the influence of drugs, and here I am.

Kaufman: Rossi was stealing things and fencing them. He killed a man following a dispute over how much he was to be paid for an electric typewriter. At his sentencing hearing, Rossi, who had no criminal history, submitted a doctor's report seeking leniency because of his addiction to cocaine. Judge Phillip Marquardt was not impressed. Just one month later the judge himself was convicted on a drug charge. Subsequently, the judge was convicted on a second marijuana charge and resigned from the bench. Rossi, who had exhausted his appeals under state law, has taken his case to federal court, challenging the judge's marijuana use and other issues.

The 54-year-old inmate says life on death row is incredibly lonely and doesn't seem to get any easier. He spends his days thinking and writing. His book, *Waiting to Die*, has been published in Europe.

Rossi: You know, we all have to reap what we sow, and we're responsible for everything we do in life. But the only problem is that lately society seems to think that we're not worth a second chance.

Kaufman: Rossi may not get a second chance. The attorney general contends that he is not entitled to a new sentencing hearing because of the Supreme Court's ruling in the so-called Ring decision.

Dennis Burke (Chief Deputy Attorney General): Do we expect litigation on those other cases? Do we expect defendants and their counsels to bring claims under Ring? Yes. But our position would be that the court said this is not retroactive.

Kaufman: But Rossi's lawyer, Dale Baich, a federal public defender, vigorously disagrees. He says he'll take the issue all the way to the Supreme Court if necessary.

Dale Baich: It would be patently unfair and arbitrary to allow re-sentencing in some cases and not in Mr. Rossi's case. The Supreme Court decision is based upon bedrock constitutional principles and, in my view, applies to all Arizona cases.

Kaufman: Meanwhile the federal court could rule that Rossi is entitled to a new sentencing hearing.

Rossi: If things go my way, I could walk out of here in a year or two. But the way things have gone, in the past 19 years, I keep getting my hopes up and they keep getting dashed, so I try to remain optimistic—you know, the half glass syndrome. But we can't always expect the results the way they come out, so I just have to go with the flow and hope for the best. Hope, that's the answer. I have to have hope.

Kaufman: Hope is something that death row inmates in nine states have more of today because of the Supreme Court ruling that juries, not judges, must make the critical decisions in deciding just who will get the death penalty. Wendy Kaufman, NPR News.

It took a very short time, three days, to pass the new sentencing law. This was in spite of testimony that the plan had flaws in it.

Arizona Supreme Court Justice, Stanley Feldman, stated that lawmakers should look at eliminating the death penalty entirely. He questioned why no one was looking at that alternative. Janet Napolitano said that she would fight any effort to put a moratorium before the voters. Her aggressive posture would prove valuable to Napolitano, who successfully ran that year for governor.

Instead of changing the sentencing law so that juries would just be determining the existence of aggravating circumstances, they overhauled the law completely to allow juries to determine both the aggravating and mitigating circumstances as well as determining whether the defendant should receive the death penalty or life in prison without the possibility of parole. By doing that, the legislature unnecessarily made Arizona's death penalty law more prone to error and bias.

The new sentencing scheme gives prosecutors two shots at getting a death sentence from a jury. If the jury determines that a defendant is guilty and unanimously agrees that no aggravating circumstances are present, a death sentence cannot be given. Rather, the judge makes the decision for life in prison, with or without the possibility of parole.

If the jury finds the defendant guilty but cannot unanimously agree that aggravating circumstances exist (which would permit the death penalty) the jury is dismissed and a second jury is empanelled to reconsider just the sentencing question. If the second jury cannot unanimously agree on an aggravating factor, leading to a death sentence, they are dismissed and the judge must order a sentence of life in prison. Allowing two different juries the opportunity to impose a death sentence obviously biases the system in favor of the death penalty. Many feel that once this new system is appealed to a higher court it will be overturned.

In the past, every death sentence was automatically reviewed by the state Supreme Court. Under the new law, that is not so. The new law reduces the Supreme Court's authority to review death sentences, limiting it to deciding whether the jury abused its discretion.

Another element of the new law concerns the mitigation specialists assigned to each case. In the past, between the time of a finding of guilt and the sentencing phase, mitigation specialists would work to build a case for mitigation of sentence based upon all of the relevant facts from the defendant's childhood to the present. That would usually take about eight months. The more mitigation factors that could be gathered and effectively presented to the court on behalf of the defendant, the better the chance to avoid the death penalty. However, under the new law the mitigation hearing is conducted the very next week after the defendant is found guilty. That will require the mitigation specialists to begin their investigation long before the case goes to trial rather than waiting to see whether a plea bargain is reached or a defendant is acquitted.

The Arizona Supreme Court has now ordered that cases must be resolved within 270 days, from arraignment to verdict, cutting the previous time into about half.

As a result of the Ring decision, two separate appeals have been taken to the Arizona Supreme Court. One by the 30 death row prisoners whose appeals were still in the state court's process, and the other by the 89 other death row prisoners whose appeals are in the federal courts. The Arizona Supreme

Court decided that the 30 appellants in the state courts would each have their sentences individually reviewed to determine whether they should be granted a new sentencing hearing due to Ring. So far, most of these cases that have been reviewed have been granted new sentencing hearings. Of course, the purpose of granting the hearing is so that a new jury can impose a new death penalty under the new law. If the review denies a new sentencing hearing the sentence must be commuted to life in prison.

When it came to the 89 other death row appeals, in February of 2003, Justice Ruth McGregor announced the decision which she wrote for the Arizona Supreme Court. She said that the US Constitution does not either forbid or require new sentencing trials. She took the position that a judge's sentence is as fair as one reached by a jury. She went on further to say that new sentencing trials would impose a substantial and unjustified burden upon the administration of justice in Arizona and that many witnesses would no longer be available to testify.

This decision appears to be arbitrary and mean spirited. It ignores the constitutional issue determined by Ring and disregards the US Supreme Court decision specifically calling for sentencing by juries. None of the reasons she offers in support of her decision bear any relevance to the issues at hand. But that is Arizona state politics. No one wants to be responsible for opening the door to the possibility that some death row prisoners may receive a new sentence less than death, or that some may even become eligible for release under the laws existing at the time they were tried.

Judges in Arizona are elected to the bench. No judge wants to appear liberal or soft on crime by allowing any prisoner to escape the death penalty, certainly not McGregor. To understand why Ruth McGregor authored such an aberrant opinion, we only need to look at her past record. She began her career as a law clerk for Supreme Court Justice Sandra Day O'Connor, and she was schooled in O'Connor's conservative ways. McGregor's opinion in the appeal based on Ring closely followed O'Connor's dissent in Ring.

Another death row prisoner, Warren Summerlin, whose case had progressed to the Federal Ninth Circuit Court, was granted an evidentiary hearing because the judge who sentenced him two decades ago was Phillip Marquardt. Summerlin and I are the only two on the row who were sentenced to death by Marquardt. At my sentencing hearing Marquardt kept falling asleep. Marquardt admitted to being addicted to marijuana during his 16 years on the bench, was forced to resign and was disbarred due to his two drug convictions. Summerlin's hearing would poke into Marquardt's private life, and no one wanted to have that judge's drug addiction dragged before the public again. Thus, the Attorney General decided to appeal for an "en banc" review before all 11 judges of the three-judge panel's decision to grant Summerlin a hearing. The court accepted the request and announced that since Summerlin had also raised the Ring issue, the court would rule on whether they felt that Ring should apply retroactively.

On September 2, 2003, the Ninth Circuit Court of Appeals announced its decision that all of approximately 100 death row prisoners, including myself, should have their death sentences vacated because Ring did apply retroactively to all of their cases, and that under the old death sentencing statutes, all prisoners should have their sentences commuted to life. That was a landmark decision because it upheld the bedrock principle that only juries may decide on a sentencing issue as important as life or death. In writing the majority opinion, Justice Sidney R. Thomas said, "deciding that judges are not constitutionally permitted to decide whether defendants are eligible for the death penalty, the Supreme Court altered the fundamental bedrock principles applicable to capital murder trials."

The issue of retroactivity at point here is a very tricky subject to explain. There are rules that govern the application of complicated and technical doctrines of newly announced constitutional principles to achieve retroactivity. Extra care is given to procedures imposing the death penalty. New substantive rules announced by the US Supreme Court generally apply retroactively, whereas new procedural principles are retroactive only if they are so major that they are considered to be, "watershed rules," that both, "alter our understanding of the bedrock procedural elements," and, "without which the likelihood of an accurate conviction is seriously diminished."

In his concurring opinion Judge Reinhardt wrote separately to say that beside the technical decisions, it is all rather straightforward. "Executing people because their cases came too early—because their appeals ended before the Supreme Court belatedly came to the realization that it had made a grievous constitutional error in its interpretation of the death penalty law, that it had erred when it failed to recognize that the United States Constitution prohibits judges, rather than jurors, from making critical factual decisions regarding life and death in capital cases—is surely arbitrariness that surpasses all bounds."

The three dissenting judges stated that the Ring decision should not be retroactive because it was neither a new substantive rule nor a fundamental alteration of a procedural one. Also, they pointed out that three other Federal Circuit Courts had ruled against Ring being retroactive.

Refusing to accept the ruling by the Ninth Circuit Court of Appeals, the state of Arizona appealed via a "writ of certiorari" to the US Supreme Court. Arizona Attorney General Terry Goddard stated that he expected the high court to reverse the case. And if the case was not reversed, the state could seek new death sentences for the 89 death row prisoners, but the process would be difficult and costly.

On June 24, 2004, the US Supreme Court rendered its decision in the Summerlin case. In a 5 to 4 vote, the court's conservatives carried the day and denied retroactivity to some 100 death row prisoners in a number of western states. This brought an end to two years of speculation, and the hopes and dreams of many.

In what has become all too familiar in Supreme Court politics, all five conservative justices blocked together their votes and overruled the four so-called liberal justices. Certainly I feel this was a political decision. There is no other justification. The court clearly ignored its own 2002 decision in the Ring case where they ruled it was improper for a sitting judge to determine the aggravating factors resulting in a death penalty. The effect was to force a change in the law so that only juries could sentence someone to death.

Writing for the court's conservative majority, Justice Scalia stated, "It does not follow that when a criminal defendant has had a full trial and one round of appeals in which the state has faithfully applied the Constitution as we understood it at the time, he may nevertheless continue to litigate his claims indefinitely in hopes that we will one day have a change of heart."

Justice Breyer, in the dissenting opinion, wrote that "the ordinary citizen will not understand" why the timing of a convicted murderer's sentencing matters."The citizen will simply witness two individuals, both sentenced through the use of unconstitutional procedures, one individual going to his death, the other saved, all through the accident of timing."

Attorney Dale Baich, an expert in defending death penalty cases, said, "it was a sad day for the Constitution." Recalling that, "the Arizona experiment of allowing a judge, sitting without a jury, to find an aggravating circumstance necessary for the imposition of the death penalty was clearly determined in Ring to violate that Sixth Amendment right." Baich also concluded that, "it certainly does not seem fair to now allow some individuals facing the death penalty a full constitutional right to a jury trial, and deny that right to others, all through the accident of timing."

The Supreme Court decision is final. All of the cases that were on hold pending this decision will now proceed to their final resolution, which for many will be the final solution of execution. Many hopes have been dashed and once again words ring hollow in a society that proclaims "justice for all." It seems that we on the row only see real justice when it is convenient or politically expedient. "Just" is a word that depends on who is defining it. To say that the only people who lost because of this decision were the prisoners on the row is to ignore the proposition that justice denied to one is justice denied to everyone.

Both Summerlin's appeal and mine will continue in the Ninth Circuit Court of Appeals, where we will both raise the issue of Judge Marquardt's incompetency due to his drug addiction and his sleeping on the bench. Hopefully an evidentiary hearing will be granted that will lead to a resentencing. But as you have seen, in this strange world of the death penalty, nothing is certain and disappointment rules the day. All we can do is to remain strong and cling to hope. For without hope, we are surely lost.

There have also been some developments regarding the execution of the mentally retarded and of juveniles. On June 22, 2002, the US Supreme Court announced in Atkins v. Virginia that it is now unconstitutional to execute the mentally retarded. For years the court has been deferential to the states on death penalty issues, but recently it has decided on a six to three vote that there appears to be a "national consensus" rejecting the use of the death penalty for the retarded as cruel and unusual punishment.

It was just 13 years ago in Penry v. Lynaugh that the same court stated that the Constitution does not bar a state from executing a mentally retarded person who was found to be competent to stand trial, whose defense of legal insanity was rejected, and who was properly convicted. Over the past 30 years since Furman v. Georgia overturned the death penalty, capital punishment advocates have seen their position supported by the court as the restrictions against executions became more and more watered down. Now we have the first important restriction on capital sentencing since Furman. It remains to be seen how strong an impact this will have on the death penalty arena, but we must rejoice and relish each victory, big or small, whenever it appears.

Now that the court has embarked down a path in which it is acknowledging the theory of "national consensus," it would seem logical to direct our attention to the issue of the execution of 16 and 17 year old juveniles. There are over 80 people on death row who committed crimes at 16 or 17 years old. The only other countries that permit the execution of juveniles are Iran, Pakistan, Nigeria, and Saudi Arabia. What strange company we keep!

It has just been announced by the US Supreme Court that they will hear a case from Missouri, Roper v. Simmons, No. 03-633, in October of 2004 that will decide again the issue of executing juveniles. Of the 38 states that use the death penalty, there are 17 who have established a minimum age of 18 for execution. That is an increase of five states since the Penry decision in 1989. Clearly, the consensus is rising against juvenile executions. In order to win this time around, it will mean that either Justice O'Connor or Justice Kennedy will have to become persuaded that the time has come to outlaw as cruel and unusual the execution of juveniles. It should not be a hard decision.

Executions will continue as long as the public is convinced that it is the correct thing to do. As long as those who seek revenge feel some satisfaction from the act, it will continue. But perhaps one day they will realize we do not replace the loss of loved ones with the brutality of the death penalty. Compounding the first brutality only adds to the suffering of the loved ones of the offender and the victim.

When one passes near death row, one can sense the presence of all those lost souls. It is like entering a living tomb. It moans, it groans, it laughs and it sighs. It is in itself a living breathing entity until it is forced to stop breathing. Death frees the dead, but not the living.

I contend that hope is the most important thing for a death row prisoner to maintain. Especially in the face of such emptiness and darkness. If we do not maintain this hope we lose the power to hold out and reduce the chance for change.

We must choose hope. It is easy to give up and hide within ourselves. To submit is to give in to fear, ignorance and apathy. I choose hope because it is a personal choice. My decision to write this book and give hope and voice to the many others on death row is a conscious choice that I hope will result in a better world.

Executions are not the solution.
Time to stop this madness.
Time to end this pain.

Man's Humanity

They say the death of one man
Diminishes us all,
But I have to wonder if that's
Really the call.

When people cry for executions
Then cheer and shout,
Have we not lost sight of what
Humanity is about?

Do we solve our problems by
Killing some more,
When killing is what we
Say we abhor.

Can we justify our pain and
Does it feel more real,
By sacrificing a poor few
Just to prove our zeal.

Have we cured the cancer
We feel so deep,
By injecting the poison
That brings eternal sleep?

And after we are sure
He is deathly still,
We then bury his body
Up on Potter's Hill.

There are no plaques to tell
Who is in eternal slumber,
Just a very small marker with
A cold lonely number.

Richard Rossi—December 1994

Appendix

The Bureaucracy of Death

Petition for Post-conviction Relief

IN THE SUPERIOR COURT FOR THE STATE OF ARIZONA
IN AND FOR THE COUNTY OF MARICOPA

STATE OF ARIZONA,	)	No. CR 135863
Plaintiff-Respondents,	)	
v.	)	PETITION FOR POST-CONVICTION RELIEF
RICHARD M. ROSSI,	)	
Defendant-Petitioner.	)	

To the Superior Court of Arizona, County of Maricopa:

Background and procedural history.

1. I am imprisoned on death row in the Arizona State Prison Eyman Complex, Special Management Unit - II ("SMU-II") at Florence, Arizona.

2. I am confined pursuant to the judgment of the Maricopa County Superior Court.

3. A jury convicted me of first degree murder, attempted first degree murder, and first degree burglary.

4. The trial judge sentenced me to death for the murder and to consecutive prison terms for the other crimes.

5. On the first direct appeal, the Arizona Supreme Court upheld my convictions and prison sentences. The Court vacated my death sentence and remanded for resentencing because it found that the "trial court did not understand the meaning and operation of the statutory scheme for finding the existence of mitigating circumstances and the evaluation and weighing of those circumstances." State v. Rossi ("Rossi I"), 146 Ariz. 359, 367-68, 706 P.2d 371, 379-80

1

(1985).

6. On remand to the same trial judge for resentencing, the trial judge again sentenced me to death despite the extensive testimony of three mental health experts all of whom recommended leniency.[1] State v. Rossi ("Rossi II"), 154 Ariz. 245, 251, 741 P.2d 1223, 1229 (1987). On

[1]Dr. Nash recommended leniency. Trial Transcript ("TR") of Presentence Hr'g, 1/17/86, pp. 5, 8-9, 18. He testified that "*had it not been* for [Rossi's] chemical dependency, his primary disease, . . . he *would not have committed the crime*." TR of Presentence Hr'g,1/17/86, pp. 16-17 [emphasis added]. Dr. Nash affirmed that I had no psychiatric illness and could "resume a perfectly normal life and be contributing as a member, not only in the prison society but on the streets." TR of Presentence Hr'g, 1/17/86, p. 17. He implored the judge to consider my disease in mitigation concluding that my offense certainly did not merit the death penalty. TR of Presentence Hr'g, 1/17/86, pp. 18, 24.

Dr. O'Connor, a Maricopa County Sheriff's Department psychiatrist, also recommended leniency. TR of Presentence Hr'g,1/17/86, pp. 27, 35-36. He testified that I had responded well to treatment for organic depression related specifically to drug dependency. TR of Presentence Hr'g, 1/17/86, pp. 30, 34. Further, he believed that I was genuinely remorseful for my actions. TR of Presentence Hr'g,1/17/86, p. 34. Although a proponent of the death penalty, Dr. O'Connor asked the judge to be lenient in my case because the progress I had made in just a short time in prison proved that I could benefit from treatment and do well. TR of Presentence Hr'g,1/17/86, pp. 35-36.

Dr. Tatro, a psychologist in private practice as a consultant, joined the other mental health experts in recommending leniency. TR of Presentence Hr'g,1/17/86, pp. 101, 115. He testified that I was intoxicated by cocaine at the time of the crime and that "when Rossi's not operating under the influence of drugs, he has a very, very strong, very conventional conscience which causes him to respect the rules and regulations of the authorities in his life." TR of Presentence Hr'g, 1/17/86, pp. 113, 121. Dr. Tatro found that "out from the influence of drugs, [Rossi] is basically a decent, well-meaning person who . . . could be of help to other inmates in a prison environment . . . [and who would like to]. . . help other people perhaps avoid some of the difficulties that he has encountered in his life." TR of Presentence Hr'g, 1/17/86, p. 115. Dr. Tatro concluded that I can be rehabilitated: "[H]e has demonstrated a capacity to succeed. . . . All the motivation is there. The ingredients are there." TR of Presentence Hr'g, 1/17/86, p. 114.

The Supreme Court also found that my cocaine addiction significantly impaired my capacity to conform my conduct to the requirements of law based on the "very persuasive Dr. Nash's *unrefuted testimony* on chemical dependency in general and how addiction fosters an insatiable and life-controlling craving for additional drugs that overwhelms the user's ability to control his physical behavior." 154 Ariz. at 251, 741 P.2d at 1229 (emphasis added). Dr. Nash testified that I was injecting cocaine at or near the time of the offense, and that my life was dominated and controlled by the drugs to the extent that *I would not have committed the crime had I not been a cocaine addict*. *Id.* at 250, 741 P.2d at 1228 (emphasis added). He further testified that my alleged statements that I was dismayed at failing to kill the neighbor, my gift of spent cartridges as souvenirs, and my delay in expressing remorse were all drug-induced behaviors. *Id.* at 249, 741 P.2d at 1227. As a result, the appellate court ordered the sentencing court on remand to consider these "two additional mitigating circumstances when imposing a new sentence." *Id.*

2

direct review, the Arizona Supreme Court again vacated the death sentence and remanded for a third sentencing.

7. In reaching its decision to remand, the Arizona Supreme Court conducted an independent review of the trial judge's findings of mitigating and aggravating circumstances,. In the Rossi II opinion it detailed that analysis for the benefit of the resentencing court. The Arizona Supreme Court approved the trial judge's finding of two aggravating factors: that the offense was committed for pecuniary gain and in a "heinous, cruel or depraved" manner. 154 Ariz. at 246, 741 P.2d at 1224. It also approved the judge's findings of proof by the preponderance of the evidence on four of the ten proffered mitigating circumstances:[2] (1) I admitted guilt and was genuinely remorseful; (2) I had no prior felony convictions and had been a responsible and productive member of society for almost my entire life; (3) I had been a model prisoner for several years; and (4) dozens of interested persons recommended leniency and attested to my good character. *Id.*

8. The Arizona Supreme Court, however, reversed the judge's conclusion that I did not

---

[2] I submitted evidence of ten mitigating factors. Three were statutory mitigating factors: (1) that my capacity to appreciate the wrongfulness of my conduct was significantly impaired by my chronic cocaine addiction (my entire personality changed; I was paranoid and suffered hallucinations); (2) that my chronic addiction also significantly impaired my capacity to conform my conduct to the requirements of the law (cocaine controlled my life, destroying my value system and instinctual controls); and (3) that I was under unusual and substantial duress (my fiancé was an alcoholic who had attempted suicide just weeks before the offense; I spent $1,000 a week on cocaine, was in financial difficulty, and had lost my job). *See* Ariz. Rev. Stat. Ann. § 13-703(G)(1)-(2).

Seven were non-statutory mitigating factors: (1) that I admitted my guilt and was genuinely remorseful for my offense; (2) that I am a good candidate for rehabilitation (supported by the testimony of three mental health experts); (3) that I had no prior felony convictions and was a responsible and productive member of society for most of my life (I worked my way through college on a scholarship; worked twelve to fifteen hours a day trying to make my grocery store a success; earned several promotions as an accountant through hard work); (4) that I am basically a compassionate, caring, giving person (dozens of friends and relatives expressed their support for me); (5) that my heavy use of cocaine the night before continued to affect me the next day and caused the offense (the effects of cocaine intoxication on personality can last for three or four days); (6) that my conduct in prison had been exemplary (no write-ups and no problems); (7) that three mental health experts unanimously recommended leniency.

3

prove by the preponderance of the evidence that he could be rehabilitated during a life sentence and that my cocaine addiction significantly impaired my capacity to conform my conduct to the requirements of law. I 154 Ariz. at 251, 741 P.2d at 1229.

9. The Supreme Court found that I could be rehabilitated based the on unanimous and uncontradicted opinion shared by three mental health experts. 154 Ariz. at 249, 741 P.2d at 1227. The appellate court found no support in the report of a state expert for the trial judge's conclusion that I could not be rehabilitated. *Id.* Finally, it found that four of the reasons given by the trial judge in support of his unfavorable conclusion had no bearing on rehabilitation. *Id.*

10. On remand for the third sentencing, a different judge presided over the presentence hearing. The Honorable Philip W. Marquardt was finally assigned to preside over my resentencing proceedings.

11. Judge Marquardt sentenced me to death.

12. On the third direct appeal, the Arizona Supreme Court affirmed the death sentence imposed by Judge Marquardt. State v. Rossi ("Rossi III"), 830 P.2d 797, 798 (1992).

13. I sought collateral relief pursuant to Ariz. R. Crim. P. 32 in the Maricopa County Superior Court. My post-conviction petition contained forty (40) claims for relief and was supported by twenty-six (26) fact specific exhibits. I also requested an evidentiary hearing.

14. The superior court denied the motion for evidentiary hearing and denied my petition seeking post-conviction relief. State v. Rossi, No. CR 135863 (Maricopa Super. Ct. Oct. 13, 1994). In so doing, and rather than reviewing each claim, the superior court simply adopted the position set forth by the state in its response to my post-conviction petition. The state's response was

4

not supported by evidence or documents outside of the trial court record.

15. I sought review of the superior court's summary dismissal of the post-conviction petition in the Arizona Supreme Court. The supreme court, through a one word entry, denied review. State v. Rossi, No. CR-95-0106-PC (Ariz. Sup. Ct. Sept. 14, 1995).

16. I then filed a Preliminary Petition for Writ of Habeas Corpus and Application for Appointment of Counsel ("Preliminary Petition") in the United States District Court for the District of Arizona. Pursuant to 28 U.S.C. § 2254 and subsequent orders issued by the district court, my First Amended Petition for Writ of Habeas Corpus Under 28 U.S.C. § 2254 by a Person in State Custody is presently pending before the United States district court.

17. I am confined unlawfully, under a conviction and death sentence which were imposed in violation of my rights under the Constitution of the United States and the Constitution of the State of Arizona, for the reasons set forth below.

First claim for relief.

> **I was denied a fair trial by an impartial jury due to failure of trial counsel to voir dire the members of the venire. This failure denied me my rights as guaranteed by the Fifth, Sixth, Eighth and Fourteenth Amendments to the United States Constitution; and Article II, Sections 4, 13, 15 and 24 of the Arizona Constitution.**

18. Trial counsel failed to conduct a voir dire the members of the venire. Counsel failed to question any of the potential jurors. In addition, counsel failed to challenge any members of the venire – including a venireperson who was a corrections officer[3] and a venireperson who previously sat as a

[3]Stella Maestas served as a corrections officer. TR 4/10/84, pp. 13-14.

5

juror in a murder case.[4]

19. The ineffectiveness of counsel during the voir dire is demonstrated by the transcript of the voir dire proceedings -- a mere forty-five (45) pages.[5]

20. Any errors which occurred during the voir dire are structural errors,[6] which require the automatic reversal of the conviction because the error infects the entire trial process by violating basic protections without which no criminal punishment may be regarded as fundamentally fair. The Court has repeatedly held that "[s]ome constitutional violations . . . by their very nature cast so much doubt on the fairness of the trial that, as a matter of law, they can never be considered harmless." Satterwhite v. Texas, 486 U.S. 249, 256 (1988). *See also* Sullivan v. Louisiana, 508 U.S. 275, 281-82 (1993) ("although most constitutional errors have been held amenable to harmless-error analysis . . . some will always invalidate the conviction."); Rose v. Clark, 478 U.S. 570, 577-578 (1986) ("some constitutional errors require reversal without regard to the evidence in the particular case . . . [because they] render a trial fundamentally unfair"); Chapman v. California, 386 U.S. 18, 23 (1967) ("there are some constitutional rights so basic to a fair trial that their infraction can never be treated as harmless error"); United States v. Olano, 507 U.S. 725, 734-35 (1993); Vasquez v. Hillery, 474 U.S. 254,

[4]Lewis McKinney previously sat as a juror in a first degree murder case. TR 4/10/84 p. 23, lines 15-19.

[5]TR 4/10/84 pp. 1-45.

[6]The Supreme Court in Brecht v. Abrahamson, 507 U.S. 619 (1993), held that the standard for assessing constitutional trial errors is harmless-error review. Trial error occurs during the presentation of case to the jury and is amenable to harmless-error analysis because it may be quantitatively assessed in the context of other evidence presented in order to determine the effect it had on the trial. Structural error affects "the entire conduct of the trial from beginning to end" as well as "the framework within which the trial proceeds." Such errors "defy analysis by 'harmless-error' standards." Arizona v. Fulminante, 499 U.S. 279, 309-310 (1991).

6

263-264 (1986).

21. The identification of any error that occurred during the voir dire phase of the proceedings are so basic to a fair trial that such infractions can never be treated as harmless error. This right includes a jury that is impartial and not organized to convict or condemn.

22. My rights as guaranteed by the Due Process Clause of the Fifth Amendment to the United States Constitution; the Right to Counsel Clause of the Sixth Amendment to the United States Constitution; the Eighth Amendment protections against cruel and unusual punishment; and the Due Process and Equal Protection Clauses of the Fourteenth Amendment to the United States Constitution, and Article II, §§ 4, 13, 15 and 24 of the Arizona Constitution were violated as a result of the failure by trial counsel to voir dire members of the venire.

Second claim for relief.

> The death penalty is applied in a racially discriminatory manner in Maricopa County, Arizona. Consideration of race in the administration of capital punishment is a violation the Eighth Amendment and the Equal Protection Clause of the Fourteenth Amendment to the United States Constitution; and Article II, Sections 4, 13, 15 and 24 of the Arizona Constitution.

23. The race of the accused and the race of the victim play a role in the selection and manner in which the criminal justice system administers capital punishment. Racism infects that system at the national, state and local levels.

24. Since the death penalty was reinstated in this country in 1976, four hundred and fifty-

7

one (451) people have been executed nationally.[7] Among those, only seven (7) white persons (1%) have been executed for killing an African-American person.[8] Of those persons executed since 1976, the victims were white in approximately eighty-three percent (83%) of the cases.[9] A 1990 study by the General Accounting Office documented a pattern of evidence indicating racial disparities in the charging, sentencing and imposition of the death penalty since Furman v. Georgia, 408 U.S. 238 (1972). "In 82% of the studies [reviewed], race of the victim was found to influence the likelihood of being charged with capital murder or receiving the death penalty, *i.e.* those who murdered whites were found more likely to be sentenced to death than those who murdered blacks."[10] Roughly half of all murder victims in this country are minorities. American society has afforded more value to a white persons life than to the life of people of color.

25. Racism is a factor in the administration of the death penalty in Arizona. The 1990 Census found that African-Americans and other persons of color make up twenty-eight percent (28%) of Arizona's population.

26. To my knowledge and belief, of the current first degree murder cases where the death penalty has been imposed in Arizona, at least one victim was white in eighty-one percent (81%) of

---

[7]Death Penalty Information Center, April, 1998.

[8]Death Penalty Information Center, April, 1998.

[9]Death Penalty Information Center, April, 1998.

[10]U.S. General Accounting Office, DEATH PENALTY SENTENCING, Feb., 1990.

8

the cases; whereas persons of color were victims in twenty-one percent (21%) of the cases.[11] In each instance in which persons of color were victims of capital murder, the defendants were also persons of color. To my knowledge and belief, there are only seven (7) cases in which the death penalty has been imposed upon white defendants when there were minority victims.[12] However, in three (3) instances, there were also white victims. This is an intolerable racial imbalance. Arizona's criminal justice system places a higher value on white victims of murder than on minority victims, while it targets minority defendants for a staggeringly disproportionate share of the death sentences.

27. The policies in effect in the Maricopa County Prosecutor's Office reflect a racial bias in charging and prosecuting capital offenses. To my knowledge and belief, of the death sentences imposed in Maricopa County, thirty-four percent (34%) of the offenders are persons of color. Approximately thirty-seven percent (37%) of Maricopa County's death sentences have been imposed against persons of color, even though, according to the 1990 Census, minorities account for approximately twenty-eight percent (28%) of Maricopa County's population.

28. Of the death sentences in Maricopa County, whites were the victims in eighty percent (80%) of the cases. Only four (4) white persons have been sentenced to death in Maricopa County in a case where the victim was a person of color. The number of minority murder victims *per capita* far exceeds the number of white murder victims *per capita*. The criminal justice system places a higher value on white victims of murder than on minority victims, while it targets persons of color for a

[11]The race of the victim is unknown in three (3) cases.

[12]Of the executions carried out in Arizona since 1992, in all cases the victims of the men executed were white.

9

staggering disproportionate share of death sentences.

29. I am White. However, a person of any race has standing to challenge policies that have a disparate impact on persons of another race. Racism in the imposition of the death penalty is the ultimate example of arbitrary, disproportionate, and cruel and unusual punishment. It is the antithesis of any evolving standard of decency. Racism makes a mockery of equal justice, equal protection and due process of law, and it can never be condoned. Any system which discriminates, either *de facto* or *de jure*, cannot withstand constitutional scrutiny.

30. My rights as guaranteed by the Due Process Clause of the Fifth Amendment to the United States Constitution; the Right to a Fair and Impartial Jury under the Sixth Amendment to the United States Constitution; the Eighth Amendment protections against cruel and unusual punishment; and the Due Process and Equal Protection Clauses of the Fourteenth Amendment to the United States Constitution, and Article II, §§ 4, 13, 15 and 24 of the Arizona Constitution were violated as a result of the policies adopted and procedures employed by the Office of the Maricopa County Prosecutor in seeking and securing a capital conviction and death sentence against me.

10

Third claim for relief.

> I will not die instantly and I will feel extreme pain and suffering as a result of an inappropriate mixture of the drugs that will be used to execute me by lethal injection. Similarly, I will not die instantly and I will feel extreme pain and suffering if I am executed by lethal gas. These forms of physical torture, as well as psychological torture, violate my right under the Eighth and Fourteenth Amendments to the United States Constitution; and Article II, Sections 4 and 25 of the Arizona Constitution.

A. Constitutional and statutory background.

31. On June 23, 1988, the Maricopa County Superior Court imposed the sentence of death upon me. At that time, the Arizona Constitution required that the sentence of death be carried out in the following manner: "[t]he judgment of death shall be inflicted by administering lethal gas."[13]

32. On November 23, 1992, the Arizona Constitution was amended to provide:

> The judgment of death shall be inflicted by administering an intravenous injection of a substance or substances in a lethal quantity sufficient to cause death except that defendants sentenced to death for offenses committed prior to the effective date of the amendment to this section shall have the choice of either lethal injection or lethal gas. . . .[14]

33. Following the amendment to the Arizona Constitution, the Arizona legislature amended Arizona Revised Statute § 13-704(B) to provide:

> A defendant who is sentenced to death for an offense committed before November 23, 1992 shall choose either lethal injection

[13]Ariz. Const. art. 22, § 22. (1933). The statutory authority providing for execution by lethal gas was contained in Arizona Revised Statute § 13-704(B).

[14]Ariz. Const. art. 22, § 22. (1992).

11

or lethal gas at least twenty days before the execution date. If the defendant fails to choose either lethal injection or lethal gas, the penalty of death shall be inflicted by lethal injection.[15]

B. Lethal injection procedure.

34. To my knowledge and belief, the following procedures will take place to cause my death by lethal injection:

35. At approximately 2:00 p.m. on the day prior to the scheduled execution, the "drugs" to be used to cause death -- prescribed by a medical doctor[16] -- will be picked up from the pharmacy

---

[15]Arizona Revised Statute § 13-704 (B) (1993).

[16]Arizona Department of Corrections (ADOC) regulations, followed by Respondents, require that a physician be present at all executions. Specifically, "[t]he Assistant Director of Health Services shall: Arrange for a physician to be present during the execution of a condemned prisoner."

ADOC regulations on executions by lethal injection require a medical doctor to take action which would assist, supervise, or contribute to the ability of another individual to cause directly the death of the condemned by mandating that a physician:

a) Monitor vital signs on site through the use of an electrocardiogram;
b) Attend and observe the execution as a physician;
c) Render technical advice regarding the execution--*i.e.* check all equipment, advise warden when all medical support devices and personnel are ready to proceed with the execution, and pronounce death;
d) Prescribe by procedure, or "chart," and supervise the injection of prescription-only, lethal drugs; and
e) Consult with and supervise lethal injection personnel as mandated by Arizona Revised Statute § 32-1491, which states that the prescribing practitioner must "provide direct supervision of a nurse or attendant involved in the dispensing process."

The procedures call for physician participation in the execution procedures. This calls for an express violation of the ethics of the profession of medicine. Every major medical society which has addressed this issue has declared physician participation in any manner, even to the examination of the inmate and determination of death, as being prohibited by the ethical standards of the medical profession.

The State of Arizona Medical Practices Acts licenses physicians to perform acts of healing, not acts of killing. Physicians have no authority to misuse the privileges granted by the medical licensure to participate in executions. The execution procedure is in conflict with this medical licensure act.

The execution procedure calls for state employees, such as the warden or his designee, to

12

at the Arizona State Prison - Florence by the Special Operations Team Leader.

36. At approximately 2:30 p.m. on the day prior to the scheduled execution, the Special Operations Team Leader and designated medical staff member will conduct an inventory of equipment and materials.

37. At approximately 4:00 p.m. on the day prior to the scheduled execution, all inventoried materials, equipment, and drugs, will be secured in the equipment area adjacent to the execution chamber.

38. At approximately 9:00 p.m. on the day prior to the scheduled execution, the executioners will arrive at Arizona State Prison - Florence.

39. At approximately 9:05 p.m. on the day prior to the scheduled execution, the "drug" box will be delivered to the warden.

---

violate federal regulations which establish restrictions on the use of controlled substances and other drugs. Sodium pentothal, Valium, morphine, Demoral and Narcan, drugs listed in the "Execution By Lethal Injection Supply Inventory" checklist, are all medications which are controlled substances under federal drug regulations and are approved only for medicinal use, not for executions.

The American Medical Association Code of Ethics strictly forbids any physician to assist in an execution. The AMA definition of assistance includes, but is not limited to, the following:

a) An action which would assist, supervise, or contribute to the ability of another individual to directly cause the death of the condemned;
b) Monitoring vital signs on sight or remotely (including monitoring electrocardiograms);
c) Attending or observing an execution as a physician;
d) Rendering technical advice regarding execution;
e) Prescribing, preparing, administering, or supervising injection drugs or their doses or types;
e) Consulting with or supervising lethal injection personnel.

ADOC policy requires a physician to prescribe and direct the administration of prescription-only drugs for use not in accord with their generally accepted therapeutic purposes. This action constitutes professional misconduct as defined by Arizona Revised Statute § 32-1401 (21)] and is grounds for disciplinary action under Arizona Revised Statute § 32-1451 A.

13

40. At approximately 9:10 p.m. on the day prior to the scheduled execution, the warden will deliver the "drug" box to the executioners.

41. At approximately 10:00 p.m. on the day prior to the scheduled execution, the Special Operations Team Restraint Team will report to the Special Operations Team Leader in the execution building security area. At about the same time either the Director of ADOC or the warden will place a telephone call to the Governor of Arizona.

42. At approximately 10:05 p.m. on the day prior to the scheduled execution, a medical doctor will arrive at the Arizona State Prison - Florence.

43. At approximately 10:30 p.m. on the day prior to the scheduled execution, a final briefing will be held with the Special Operations Restraint Team by the Special Operations Team Leader.

44. At approximately 11:00 p.m. on the day prior to the scheduled execution, the warden will give the signal to proceed.

45. At approximately 11:05 p.m. on the day prior to the scheduled execution, the Special Operations Team Restraint Team will remove me from my cell, conduct a strip search, and escort me to the execution chamber. At that time the Director of ADOC will ask me if I have any last words.

46. At approximately 11:30 p.m. on the day prior to the scheduled execution, the restraint of me will be completed and the Special Operations Team will exit the execution chamber.

47. Between 11:35 and 11:55 p.m. on the day prior to the scheduled execution, the executioners will insert the "IV's," into my arms and a heart monitor will be positioned on my chest.

48. At approximately 11:55 p.m. on the day prior to the scheduled execution, the witnesses to the execution will be admitted to the witness observation area.

14

49. At approximately 12:02 a.m. on the day of the scheduled execution, a medical examiner will be admitted to the staging area and the warden will give a signal that the witnesses are in place.

50. At approximately 12:03 a.m. on the day of the scheduled execution, the Director of ADOC may tell the witnesses that there has been no reprieve.

51. At approximately 12:04 am on the day of the scheduled execution, the Director of ADOC tells the warden to proceed and the Special Operations Team Leader will exit the execution chamber. After a thirty (30) second wait, the blinds to the witness area will be opened.

52. At approximately 12:05 am on the day of the scheduled execution, the warden will tell the executioners to proceed and the execution will commence.

53. At approximately 12:10 am on the day of the execution, the executioners will notify the warden when the execution is completed. The warden will await a signal from the medical doctor that the heart monitor indicates my death.

54. At approximately 12:20 am on the day of execution, the blinds to the witness area will be closed. The medical examiner will be admitted to the execution chamber.

55. At approximately 12:25 am on the day of the execution, either the Director of ADOC or the warden will advise the witnesses that the execution was completed.

C. Drugs.

56. To my knowledge and belief, the following drugs will be used to cause my death: Pentothal; Pancuronium (Pavulon™) and Potassium Chloride. In addition, Valium, Lidocaine HCL, Epinephrine, Xylocaine, Narcan, Morphine and Demoral are available for use during the lethal injection process. Of these drugs, Pentothal, Valium, Narcan, Morphine and Demoral, are all

15

medications which are controlled substances under federal drug regulations and are approved only for medicinal use, not for executions. Possession and use of these drugs is restricted to individuals properly licensed by the Internal Revenue Service for use of these controlled substances.

57. Pentothal, Pancuronium, and Potassium Chloride are prescription-only drugs as defined by Arizona Revised Statute §32-1901 (57)a, which provides: "[a]ny drug which because of its toxicity or other potentiality for harmful effect, or the method of its use, or the collateral measures necessary to its use, is not generally recognized among experts . . . , as safe for use except by or under the supervision of a medical practitioner."

58. The "prescription-only drugs" that will be used to cause my death will not be used for the intended therapeutic value.

59. Section 32-1968 of the Arizona Revised Statutes mandates that, "A prescription-only drug shall be dispensed only . . . (1) [by] a medical practitioner in conformance with § 32-1921; (2) Upon a written prescription order;[17] (3) Upon an oral prescription order. . . ; [or] (4) By renewing any such written or oral prescription order. . . .

60. Respondents engage in a practice whereby the "prescription-only drugs" used in lethal injection executions are dispensed upon a prescription procedure identified as "charting." The "charting" procedure is a prescription order, necessarily made by a medical doctor, which is entered into the condemned prisoner's medical "chart." After "charting" is complete, Respondents allow for the drugs to be dispensed to the Special Operations Team Leader and administered by the

[17]Arizona Revised Statute § 32-1901 (58) a and b, define in pertinent part, a prescription order as (1) "An order to a pharmacist for drugs or devices issued and signed by a duly licenced medical practitioner in the authorized course of his professional practice;" or (2) "An order transmitted to a pharmacist through word of mouth, telephone or other means of communication directed by such medical practitioner."

16

executioners at the execution.

61. Under Arizona Revised Statute § 32-1491(D), the prescribing practitioner, in this case a medical doctor, must "provide direct supervision of a nurse or attendant involved in the dispensing process."

D. Previous executions by lethal injection in Arizona.

62. In 1976, the United States Supreme Court permitted the states to again carry out executions. Gregg v. Georgia, 428 U.S. 153 (1976). Since that time, Arizona has executed nine (9) individuals. Eight (8) of the nine (9) men were executed by lethal injection.

63. On April 6, 1992, Donald Gene Harding was executed by lethal gas. His execution will be described later.

64. On March 3, 1993, John George Brewer was executed by lethal injection. Mr. Brewer waived his appeals. To my knowledge and belief, the first drug administered to Mr. Brewer was pentothal. The intended effect of this drug was to sedate Mr. Brewer. The anesthesia-inducing actions of pentothal are of very brief duration. A subject awakens rapidly from its effects. It is classified as an ultra short-acting barbiturate. Recovery from the effects of this drug, which has occurred when completion of execution has been prolonged, subjects the inmate to suffering and torture because of the painful sensations of suffocation produced by the paralyzing effects of Pancuronium and the extreme sensation of burning produced by potassium chloride. The level of pentothal listed in the autopsy report is well below the therapeutic range.

65. On April 14, 1993, James Dean Clark was executed by lethal injection. To my knowledge and belief, the first drug administered to Mr. Clark was pentothal. The intended effect of this drug was to sedate Mr. Clark. The anesthesia-inducing actions of sodium pentothal are of very

17

brief duration. A subject awakens rapidly from its effects. It is classified as an ultra short-acting barbiturate. Recovery from the effects of this drug, which has occurred when completion of execution has been prolonged, subjects the inmate to suffering and torture because of the painful sensations of suffocation produced by the paralyzing effects of Pancuronium and the extreme sensation of burning produced by potassium chloride. The level of pentothal listed in the autopsy report is well below the therapeutic range.

66. On September 13, 1995, Jimmie Wayne Jeffers was executed by lethal injection. I do not presently possess information to describe the execution of Mr. Jeffers.

67. On June 19, 1996, Darren Bolton was executed by lethal injection. Mr. Bolton waived his appeals. I do not presently possess information to describe the execution of Mr. Bolton.

68. Luis Mata was executed on August 22, 1996. Under established procedures, Mata was strapped to a gurney at approximately 11:30 pm. on August 21st and the lethal injection needles were inserted. To my knowledge and belief, Mr. Mata remained in this position in the execution chamber for one hour and ten minutes while his attorneys were arguing to the Arizona Supreme Court.[18]

69. When the execution went forward, the following occurred:

> All of a sudden, the praying stopped. Immediately, Mr. Mata's head jerked back and from side to side several times. Then, his face contorted.
>
> Then, his mouth and lips flapped in a very unnatural way

[18]This is not the only instance of an inmate being strapped to the gurney with the lethal needle in his arm. For instance, on January 8, 1997, Kirt Wainwright was strapped to a gurney with the needle inserted in his arm for forty-five minutes while the United States Supreme Court considered his appeal. Rick Bragg, *An Evening of Death, Punishment for 3 Murderers*, THE NEW YORK TIMES, January 10, 1997 at A1.

18

> -- sort of like one does when one is exhausted and says "phew" or sort of like when one makes a raspberry sound, but more extreme and unnatural and involving the entire mouth area instead of just his lips. . . .
>
> Mr. Mata's body stopped moving, and I thought it was over. I was watching Mr. Mata at this time and not my watch, so I do not know exactly how much time passed, but it seemed like a couple of minutes.
>
> Then, his chest and stomach began quick, sharp heaving. His chest and stomach went up and down about six or seven times. Then, he did not move.
>
> The execution was not like going to sleep. There were several contortions and jerks in the body, such that I cannot get the picture of them out of my mind. Because the execution chamber is soundproof, I do not know what sounds were made as Mr. Mata was dying.[19]

70. Randy Greenawalt was executed on January 23, 1997. Under established procedures, Mr. Greenawalt was strapped to a gurney at approximately 11:30 pm. and the lethal injection needles were inserted.

71. When the execution went forward, the following occurred:

> In the center of the far wall, behind Randy, was a large pane of one-way glass. Below it was a small rectangular opening obscured by a curtain. A black tube led from the opening. I presume it branched in two for both of Randy's arms, I could really discern only that his near arm was intubated.
>
> There was a slight movement of the small curtain which must have coincided with the first drug, the sodium pentothal, and Randy reacted almost immediately. He turned his head away from the viewing area and looked straight up at the ceiling and never looked our way again. His feet continued their gentle

[19] Affidavit by Jeffery L. Kirchmeier, Jan. 10, 1997 ("Kirchmeier Affidavit"). *See also* Steve Benson, *Bearing witness to a wrongful execution*, THE ARIZONA REPUBLIC., Sept. 1, 1996 at B1.

19

churning and he visibly tensed.

A slight movement in the small curtain on the far wall caught my attention again and the Pavulon was sent to Randy's veins. His feet came to a stop. His breathing, unremarkable up to now, changed markedly. He exhaled twice in succession through loosely pursed lips; they literally fluttered. After a pause, his already large belly expanded twice, then, after a brief pause, a third time. That was the last I could discern him breathing.

For the third time the little curtain foretold the next injection. At first nothing at all seemed to happen, then Randy's entire body lurched, straining against the leather. In fairly rapid succession he sustained three of these full-body spasms. These were entirely unexpected and took me aback. Randy then lay still for a moment and I thought the process complete when I was startled by a fourth. My sense was that if he had not been lashed to the table, he would have lifted entirely off the surface. I believe Randy tensed most, if not all his muscles and that he was trying to arch backwards, perhaps to burst the restraints. Those were Randy Greenawalt's last physical movements.

Randy lay on the table for a time and the witnesses stood in complete silence and stared. After a time I could see the color recede from Randy's face; it is then, I remain convinced, that life left his body. We stood a bit longer, still in utter silence, staring at Randy's remains, until some unseen person closed the curtain.[20]

72. On June 25, 1997 William Woratzeck was executed by lethal injection. I do not presently possess information to describe the execution of Mr. Woratzeck.

73. Jose Jesus Ceja was executed on January 21, 1998. Under established procedures, Mr. Ceja was strapped to a gurney at approximately 11:30 pm. and the lethal injection needles were inserted.

[20]Affidavit by Jeffry Kelleher ("Kelleher Affidavit").

20

74. When the execution went forward, the following occurred:

> This is what the Arizona Department of Corrections did to Jose Jesus Ceja. I was there.
>
> * * * . .
>
> They led him to a gurney in the execution chamber and strapped him down. Then they put catheters into the veins of his arms. They may or may not have had to dissect an arm -- with the inmate fully conscious -- in order to find the correct veins. When this is necessary, they call it "cutting down." They left him lying like that for about a half-hour, and then, when they knew there had been no last-minute reprieve, they gave the order to open the curtain that hid him from the view of the witnesses -- the inmate's witnesses, state's witnesses and journalists. No "victim's witnesses" -- members of the Leons' family -- attended.
>
> When the curtain opens, Ceja looks like a man tucked cozily in bed. It's a cosmetic maneuver worthy of an advertising agency. Witnesses weren't allowed to see him being strapped down, or his arms being pierced by needles. Because of the sheet that's tucked around him, and the strategic positioning of the gurney, there's no indication that he has needles in his arms. There's no sign of any tubes or catheters.
>
> I have the best -- or worst -- view a witness can have. Because I was invited by Ceja, I'm standing right down at the front. . . .
>
> * * *
>
> When the order comes to open the curtain, and a guard does it, I almost recoil. I'd imagined there would be some distance, that it would all be far away. But I'm standing so close to Ceja that, if it weren't for the soundproof window, we could hold a conversation without having to raise our voices.
>
> * * *
>
> When he realizes the curtain has been removed, he raises his head and looks at the witnesses. . . .
>
> Terry Stewart, the DOC's director, enters the death room and

21

> stands beside Ceja. An intercom system is turned on, and we hear Stewart ask Ceja if he has anything he wants to say.
>
> "No," Ceja answers, his voice tinged with a Mexican accent.
>
> Stewart asks him if he's waiving his right to say anything.
>
> "That's right," Ceja answers. His manner is calm, his tone of voice flat but not hostile.
>
> Stewart exits. Then Meg Savage, warden of Florence prison, comes in and reads Ceja his death warrant. He lies there impassively as she does. Then she leaves, and Ceja is killed.
>
> We can't see it happen, but he's injected with Pentothal, an ultra-short-acting sedative. Then Pancuronium, which paralyzes every voluntary muscle in the body. The purpose of this is to make death look peaceful -- even if the inmate is in intense pain, he won't be able to show it. Finally, they inject him with potassium chloride, which stops the heart.
>
> Nothing changes in the death room, except for Ceja. He closes his eyes, and his breathing gets quicker. His face goes into spasm, as though there's an explosion going on just under his skin. His upper lip trembles and then billows out from his face, like a rag flapping in a strong wind. . . . After a minute or so -- or maybe longer, I don't know -- Ceja is just lying there. I look for signs of breathing and don't see any. Then the order comes to close the curtain, and the guard does. There's no announcement that Ceja is dead, just the order to close the curtain.[21]

75. The Eighth Amendment prohibits methods of carrying out the death sentence that involve the "unnecessary and wanton infliction of pain," unneeded terror or disgrace, or "lingering death." Gregg v. Georgia, 428 U.S. 153, 173 (1976); Louisiana ex rel Francis v. Resweber, 329 U.S. 459, 463 (1947); In re Kemmler, 136 U.S. 436 (1890); Wilkerson v. Utah, 99 U.S. 130

[21]Barry Graham, *Witness at an execution: Graham watches as the state gets away with murder*, PHOENIX NEW TIMES, Feb. 5-11, 1998 at 15.

22

(1879). The lethal injection method of execution to be used by Arizona in this case, and as applied to me, violates this fundamental constitutional mandate.

E. Lethal injection causes pain.

76. My death will not be immediate.

77. Arizona's death penalty scheme currently requires that the condemned be put to death "by administering an intravenous injection of a substance or substances in a lethal quantity sufficient to cause death . . . ."[22] However, the method devised by the Respondents entails a substantial risk of gratuitous, torturous pain and prolonged suffering and thus violates the Eighth Amendment.

78. To my knowledge and belief, Respondents have not devised a set of written standards or procedures to be followed by the executioners in carrying out an execution.

79. The procedure, with its absence of guidelines and instructions and failure to require the executioners to be properly trained, increases the risk of error and unnecessary pain and prolonged suffering many times over.

80. The heightened fear that I will experience while strapped and hooked up to the lethal needle for a period of thirty-five (35) minutes -- waiting to die -- before the execution can even go forward, will cause psychological suffering by, and torture of, me.

81. The executioners, who are unskilled personnel, may be unable to insert successfully an IV catheter into me.[23] The insertion of the catheter can be extremely difficult, especially if I have

[22]Ariz. Const. art. 22, § 22. (1992).

[23]To carry out the execution, the preparations to insert the lethal needle begin thirty-five (35) minutes before the stated time for the execution. An IV placement is a procedure which ordinarily is complete within 3 to 5 minutes. If a surgical cut-down procedure is required -- meaning that the executioners need to dissect me in order to insert the IV -- it should be completed by competent medical personnel within 10 to 15 minutes.

23

constricted veins due to the stress of the impending execution. It is quite likely that my anxiety in the minutes leading up to the execution will cause constriction of my veins. If the catheter is not properly inserted, there is a risk that the chemicals will be injected into my muscle and other tissue rather than directly into my bloodstream, causing extreme pain in the form of a severe burning sensation. Furthermore, a failure to inject the chemicals directly into the bloodstream will cause the chemicals to be absorbed far more slowly, and the intended effect of sedation will not occur.

82. Improper insertion of the IV catheter into me could also result in its falling out of the vein, resulting in a failure to inject the intended dosage of chemicals. There is also a risk that the catheter will rupture or leak as pressure builds up during the administration of the chemicals unless the catheter has adequate strength and all the joints and connections are adequately reinforced.

83. The Arizona lethal injection protocol allows for severe risks of error in the complicated set-up procedure. There is no procedure for the labeling of the syringes in which the various chemicals and saline solution are to be placed. Unless labeled or otherwise marked, the syringes are almost completely indistinguishable. Mistakes in this process would result in the chemicals being administered to me in the wrong sequence would cause extreme torture, suffering and pain.

84. There have been other instances of an inmate being strapped to the gurney with the executioner attempting to insert the lethal needle in their arms.[24] In one case,

> The execution team began trying to find a veins in each arm at 12:14 a.m. and continued until 12:30 a.m. according to DOC records.

---

[24]Rick Bragg, *An Evening of Death, Punishment for 3 Murderers,* THE NEW YORK TIMES, January 10, 1997 at A1.

24

> At that point the doctor was called in and gave [Tommie] Smith a local anesthetic. Then he tried to insert the tube in his neck.
>
> When that failed he was able to insert the angiocath in Smith's foot completing the procedure at 12:55 a.m.
>
> ...
>
> "he just laid there very still with his eyes closed," [prison spokeswoman] Pattison said.[25]

85. To my knowledge and belief, respondents do not have in place rules or regulations to ensure that executioners are properly and sufficiently trained to handle the technical aspects of the execution, *i.e.*, the insertion of needles and catheters, the preparation of the lethal substances, the determination of proper dosage and sequence of the drugs, etc. Respondents do not require that executioners have any level of medical training or competency. Respondents do not provide any written guidelines or instructions to the executioners regarding the preparation of the drugs, the intravenous injection, the sequence of the drugs, or the determination of proper dosage.

86. The procedures employed by respondents do not take into account my body weight in accounting for the amount of "drugs" that the executioners will administer. I will *unquestionably* experience pain as a result of the practices of respondents in not considering the body weight in determining the amount of lethal "drugs" to administer to me. "Even a slight error in dosage or administration can leave a prisoner conscious but paralyzed while dying, a sentient witness of his or her own slow, lingering asphyxiation." Chaney v. Heckler, 718 F.2d 1174, 1191 (D.C. Cir. 1983), *rev'd on other grounds*, 470 U.S. 821 (1985).

[25]Sherri Edwards and Suzanne McBride, *Doctor's aid in injection violated ethics rules*, THE INDIANAPOLIS STAR, Jul. 19, 1996 at A1.

25

87. At the very least, written standards and procedures are necessary to minimize the risk of error. The requisite written instructions and guidelines would indicate the proper methods for determining appropriate dosage and for setting up the IV. Further, written instructions would set forth the requisite training and qualifications for the technicians. The failure to provide such instruction and established procedure combined with the failure to require that the execution technicians be trained and certified amounts to nothing short of unauthorized, unethical and inhumane treatment of me.

88. Death "where unconsciousness is likely to be immediate or within a matter of seconds is apparently within constitutional limits . . . the persistence of consciousness for over a minute or between a minute and a minute-and-a-half, but no longer than two minutes might be outside of constitutional boundaries." Fierro v. Gomez, 77 F.3d 301, 308 (9th Cir.) *vacated on other grnd's* ___ U.S. ___, 117 S.Ct. 285 (1996) (remanded for reconsideration in light of changing statute). A method is unconstitutional if I face a "substantial risk" of suffering "extreme pain for several minutes." *Id.* This risk is heightened if the execution protocol is created in an "unscientific, slapdash manner." Fierro v. Gomez, 865 F. Supp. 1387, 1413 (N.D. Cal. 1994) *aff'd*, 77 F.3d 301.

F. Lethal gas.

89. Execution by cyanide gas is in essence asphyxiation by suffocation or strangulation.[26]

90. On April 6, 1992, Arizona executed Don Eugene Harding.

> When the fumes enveloped Don's head he took a quick breath. A few seconds later he again looked in my direction. His face was red and contorted as if he were attempting to fight through

[26] Gomez v. United States District Court, 503 U.S. 653, 655 (1992) (Stevens and Blackmun, JJ., dissenting).

26

> tremendous pain. His mouth was pursed shut and his jaw was clenched tight. Don then took several more quick gulps of the fumes.
>
> At this point Don's body started convulsing violently. . . . His face and body turned a deep red and the veins in his temple and neck began to bulge until I thought they might explode.
>
> After about a minute Don's face leaned partially forward, but he was still conscious. Every few seconds he continued to gulp in. He was shuddering uncontrollably and his body was racked with spasms. His head continued to snap back. His hands were clenched.
>
> After several more minutes, the most violent of the convulsions subsided. At this time the muscles along Don's left arm and back began twitching in a wavelike motion under his skin. Spittle drooled from his mouth. . . .
>
> Don did not stop moving for approximately eight minutes, and after that he continued to twitch and jerk for another minute. Approximately two minutes later, we were told by a prison official that the execution was complete.
>
> Don Harding took ten minutes and thirty one seconds to die.[27]

91. The unnecessary cruelty of this method of execution convinced Arizona's Attorney General that the state should abandon execution by gas in favor of execution by lethal injection. His conclusion coincides with that of numerous medical, legal, and ethical experts.[28]

92. Execution by lethal gas is unconstitutional under the Eighth and Fourteenth Amendments.[29]

---

[27] Gomez v. United States District Court, 503 U.S. at 655-56.

[28] Gomez v. United States District Court, 503 U.S. at 655-56.

[29] Fierro v. Gomez, 77 F.3d 301, 309 (9th Cir.) *vacated on other grnd's* ___ U.S. ___, 117 S.Ct. 285 (1996) (remanded for reconsideration in light of changing statute).

27

G. Choice of method of execution.

93. The method of execution specified by Arizona Constitution and state statutes at the time of my death sentence was death by lethal gas.

94. By a constitutional amendment dated November 3, 1992, the method of carrying out a death sentence was changed in Arizona from death by lethal gas to death by lethal injection. The Amendment, which became effective on November 23, 1992, gives those defendants sentenced to death prior to its enactment the option of choosing death by gas or injection.

95. The *Ex Post Facto Clause* of the United States Constitution, Article I, § 10, is based upon the notion that persons have a right to fair warning of that conduct which will give rise to a criminal penalty and what this penalty consists of. A law violates the *Ex Post Facto Clause* if it makes more burdensome the punishment for a crime after its commission.

96. The Constitutional Amendment at issue imposes a new penalty of death by lethal injection in the event that I do not choose death by lethal gas. This change violates the *Ex Post Facto Clause*. The new law further violates the *Ex Post Facto Clause* with respect to me because it materially changes and increases the sentence pronounced on me by requiring me to choose the method of execution to be applied to me. Such infliction amounts to a greater punishment by making me an active participant in my own execution.

97. The Constitutional Amendment and proposed legislation further violate my Due Process rights under the Fourteenth Amendment to the United States Constitution as they alter my sentence without any opportunity for judicial hearing.

98. Alternatively, assuming the Constitutional Amendment and the proposed legislation can

28

alter the State Court's prior sentence of death by lethal gas, it is cruel and unusual punishment to require me to choose my own method of execution, in violation of the Eighth Amendment.

H. Conclusion

99. Application of the execution of the sentence of death by lethal injection or lethal gas upon me will violate my right to be free from cruel and unusual punishment as guaranteed by the Eighth and Fourteenth Amendments to the United States Constitution, and , and Article II, §§ 4 and 25 of the Arizona Constitution.

Fourth claim for relief.

> The Arizona Death Penalty Statute violates Article VI of the United States Constitution and various international laws including, but not limited to, the Organization of American States Treaty and the American Declaration of the Rights and Duties of Man; and Article II, Section 3 of the Arizona Constitution.

100. Pursuant to the Supremacy Clause of Article VI of the United States Constitution, the judges of every state are bound by the terms of international treaties to which the United States of America ("United States") is a party, "anything in the constitution or laws of any State to the contrary notwithstanding."

101. The United States is a member nation and signatory to the Organization of American States ("OAS")Treaty. Pursuant to that treaty, the United States is bound by the terms of the American Declaration of the Rights and Duties of Man.

102. The American Declaration of the Rights and Duties of Man provides in part:

> Article I. Every human being has the right to life, liberty and the security of his person.
>
> Article II. All persons are equal before the law and have the rights

29

and duties established in this declaration, without distinction as to race, sex, language, creed or any other factor.

Article XVIII. Every person may resort to the courts to ensure respect for his legal rights. There should likewise be available to him a simple, brief procedure whereby courts will protect him from acts of authority that, to his prejudice, violate any fundamental constitutional rights.

Article XXV. No person may be deprived of his liberty except in the cases and according to the procedures established by preexisting laws.

No person may be deprived of liberty for nonfulfillment of obligations of a purely civil character.

Every individual who has been deprived of his liberty has the right to have the legality of his detention ascertained without delay by a court, and the right to be tried without undue delay or, otherwise, to be released. He also has the right to humane treatment during the time he is in custody.

Article XXVI. Every accused person is presumed to be innocent until proved guilty.

Every person who is accused of an offense has the right to be given an impartial and public hearing, and to be tried by courts previously established in accordance with preexisting laws, and not to receive cruel, infamous or unusual punishment.

103. The right of life is guaranteed by Article I of the American Declaration of the Rights and Duties of Man. With one exception, no party to the OAS Charter has re-instituted the death penalty for any crime once it has been abolished within that state. Seventeen of the thirty-one member states have agreed under the American Convention on Human Rights not to do so. *See* Amer. Conv. H. Rts. Chapter II, Articles 4(2) and 4(3). ("The death penalty shall not be re-established in states that have abolished it.")

104. The United States is a signatory to the American Convention on Human Rights

30

(November 22, 1969) and as such is prohibited, pursuant to the Vienna Convention on the Law of Treaties, Article 18(a) (executed May 23, 1969) from doing any act that would defeat the object and purpose of the treaty. One obvious and fundamental purpose of the OAS Charter is safe-guarding the right to human life. Moreover, it is clear that the OAS Charter and Article I of the American Declaration express the intention that signatory states *not* re-institute the death penalty once it has been abolished in that state. Because the death penalty was judicially abolished in the United States in 1972 in Furman v. Georgia, 408 U.S. 238 (1972), under the American Declaration, the OAS Charter, the American Convention on Human Rights, the Vienna Convention, and Article IV of the U.S. Constitution, the federal government and the individual states, through the Supremacy Clause, cannot reimpose the death penalty.

105. In addition, it is the custom and practice of civilized nations not to reimpose the death penalty once it has been abolished. The practices of nations determine international customary law. As discussed above, no other OAS member has successfully reimposed the death penalty once abolished. Throughout the world, most Pacific, European, Central and South American and African nations do not use the death penalty. Indeed, one hundred and one (101) countries have abolished the death penalty in law or practice. [30] Another fifty-seven (57) countries have abolished the death

[30]The following countries have abolished the death penalty for all crimes: Andorra, Angola, Australia, Austria, Cambodia, Cape Verde, Colombia, Costa Rica, Croatia, the Czech Republic, Denmark, the Dominican Republic, Ecuador, Finland, France, Germany, Greece, Guinea-Bissau, Haiti, Honduras, Hong Kong, Hungary, Iceland, Ireland, Italy, Federal Republic of Kiribati, Liechtenstein, Luxembourg, Macedonia, Marshall Islands, Mauritius, Micronesia, Moldova, Monaco, Mozambique, Namibia, the Netherlands, New Zealand, Nicaragua, Norway Palau, Panama, Poland, Portugal, Romania, San Marino, Sao Tome and Principe, Slovak Republic, Slovenia, Solomon Islands, Spain, Sweden, Switzerland, Tuvalu, Uruguay, Vanuatu, Vatican City State, Venezuela. Fifteen countries retaining the death penalty uniquely for exceptional crimes and which have abolished it for all ordinary crimes: Argentina, Brazil, Canada, Cyprus, El Salvador, Fiji,

31

penalty for all crimes. Further, fifteen (15) have abolished it for all ordinary crimes retaining it for exceptional circumstances such as crimes committed under military law or during wartime. Finally, twenty-eight (28) countries can be considered abolitionist in practice in that they have not executed anyone over the last ten years. [31]

106. Of the ninety-four (94) other countries that retain and use the death penalty, in practice the number of executions in any one year is much smaller. The majority that retain the death penalty are either Islamic or the former Soviet Union, and feature some of the most totalitarian political systems in the world with the worst record of human rights abuses (*e.g.* Iraq, Saudi Arabia, Kenya, Algeria, China). Moreover, the United Nations and the Council of Europe have clearly indicated their expectations that member nations will abolish the death penalty. *See* United Nations Charter Articles 55 and 56; International Covenant on Civil and Political Rights; the Convention for the Protection of Human Rights and Fundamental Freedoms, Concerning the Abolition of the Death Penalty, European Treaty Series No. 114, May 1983. The United Nations is currently in the process of drafting a General Assembly resolution against the death penalty. Furthermore, it is a pre-requisite for countries wishing to join the European Union that they make a commitment to abolish their death penalty. All members have abolished it for all crimes.[32]

Israel, Malta, Mexico, Nepal, Paraguay, Peru, Seychelles, South Africa, United Kingdom.

[31]These nations include: Albania, Belgium, Bermuda, Bhutan, Bolivia, Brunei Darussalam, Burundi, Central African Republic, the Congo, Comoros, Cote d'Ivoire, Djibouti, Gambia, Madagascar, Maldives, Mali, Nauru, Niger, Papua New Guinea, the Philippines, Rwanda, Senegal, Suriname, Sri Lanka, Togo, Tonga, Turkey, Western Samoa.

[32]With the exception of Belgium and the U.K., which have eliminated it in practice.

International human rights treaties prohibit anyone under the age of eighteen (18) at the time of the crime from being sentenced to death. The International Covenant on Civil and Political Rights, the American Convention on Human Rights and the UN Convention on the Rights of the Child all have provisions to this effect. More than one hundred (100) countries have laws specifically excluding the executions of juvenile offenders. Only five countries are known to have executed prisoners who were juveniles at the time of their crime since 1990: Iran, Pakistan, Saudi Arabia, Yemen and the United States, which has carried out six (6) executions, the majority.

107. I have been denied my rights under the American Declaration of the Rights and Duties of Man as applicable to the State of Arizona through the Supremacy Clause for the following reasons and such other reasons as may come to light:

a) I was subjected to arbitrary deprivation of my right to life as prohibited under Article I of the American Declaration because the death penalty in Arizona is imposed in a racially discriminatory manner in violation of Article II of the American Declaration of the Rights and Duties of Man and Article 3 of the OAS Charter.

b) The death penalty is a cruel, infamous and unusual punishment resulting in the arbitrary deprivation of life when it is applied in a racially discriminatory manner, in the absence of an impartial hearing and equality before the law in violation of Article XXVI of the American Declaration of the Rights and Duties of Man.

c) I was denied equal treatment before the law as guaranteed under Article II of the American Declaration of the Rights and Duties of Man because I was denied the opportunity to be tried by an impartial jury as a result of the death qualification process.

108. The sentence of death denies me my rights as guaranteed by the American Declaration of the Rights and Duties of Man, The Organization of American States Charter and Article VI of the United States Constitution; and Article II, § 3 of the Arizona Constitution.

33

Prayer for relief.

WHEREFORE, I respectfully pray that this Court:

a) Order that I be granted leave to conduct discovery;

b) Order that upon completion of discovery, I be granted leave to amend the instant petition;

c) Order that respondent file an answer or other responsive pleading to my amended petition;

d) Grant an evidentiary hearing at which proof may be offered concerning the allegations of this petition;

e) Have me brought before it to the end that I may be discharged from my unconstitutional confinement and restraint;

f) In the alternative issue an order to have me brought before it to the end that I may be relieved of my unconstitutional sentences;

g) Grant such other relief as may be appropriate and to dispose of the matter as law and justice require.

Respectfully submitted this ___ day of April, 1998.

By:______________________
Richard M. Rossi, *pro se*
50337
Arizona State Prison-Florence
P.O. Box 3400
Florence, Arizona 85232

A copy of the foregoing mailed this ___ day of April, 1998 to Diane M. Ramsey, Assistant Attorney General, 1275 W. Washington, Phoenix, AZ 85007-2997.

By:______________________
Richard M. Rossi, *pro se*
50337

34

Warrant of Execution

FILED
JUN 25 1996
NOEL K. DESSAINT
CLERK SUPREME COURT
BY

SUPREME COURT OF ARIZONA

STATE OF ARIZONA, Appellee, vs. RICHARD MICHAEL ROSSI, Appellant.	Supreme Court No. CR-88-0302-AP Maricopa County No. CR-135863 **WARRANT OF EXECUTION**

The appeal in the above-entitled cause was heard and fully considered by this Court on the 8th day of November, 1990, and having finally decided the cause, this Court on the 2nd day of April, 1992, did affirm the judgment of the Superior Court of Maricopa County, State of Arizona, and did file its opinion, which opinion is now of record in this Court, is still in effect, and, as shown by this Court's record, has not been stayed or affected by any subsequent decision of this or any other Court.

WHEREAS, the Attorney General having filed a Request for Warrant of Execution, which was granted by this Court on the 19th day of June, 1996,

NOW THEREFORE, IT IS ORDERED, that Wednesday, the 24th day of July, 1996, be and the same is hereby fixed as the time when the judgment and sentence of death pronounced upon the appellant, RICHARD MICHAEL ROSSI, by the Superior Court of Maricopa County, State of Arizona, shall be executed by administering to RICHARD MICHAEL ROSSI an intravenous injection of a substance or substances in a lethal quantity sufficient to cause death, except that RICHARD MICHAEL ROSSI shall have the choice of either lethal injection or lethal gas.

Supreme Court No. CR-88-0302-AP
WARRANT OF EXECUTION
Page Two

IT IS FURTHER ORDERED that the Clerk of this Court forthwith prepare and certify under his hand and the seal of this Court a full, true and correct copy of this Warrant, and cause the same to be delivered to the Director of the Department of Corrections and the Superintendent of the State Prison, at Florence, Arizona, and the same shall be sufficient authority to them for the execution of the appellant, RICHARD MICHAEL ROSSI, as commanded by the judgment and sentence of death pronounced against RICHARD MICHAEL ROSSI, by the Superior Court of Maricopa County, State of Arizona, on the 23rd day of June, 1988.

Upon the execution of RICHARD MICHAEL ROSSI, the Superintendent shall, pursuant to Rule 31.17(c), Rules of Criminal Procedure, forthwith make a return upon this Warrant to the Supreme Court of Arizona, which return shall show the time, mode and manner of execution.

Dated in the City of Phoenix, Arizona, at the Arizona Courts Building, this 25th day of June, 1996.

STANLEY G. FELDMAN, Chief Justice

THOMAS A. ZLAKET, Vice Chief Justice

JAMES MOELLER, Justice

FREDERICK J. MARTONE, Justice

Arizona Board of Clemency: Notification Letter

FIFE SYMINGTON
GOVERNOR

MICHAEL D. GARVEY
EXECUTIVE DIRECTOR

ARIZONA
BOARD OF EXECUTIVE CLEMENCY

1645 WEST JEFFERSON
SUITE 326
PHOENIX, ARIZONA 85007
(602) 542-5656
FAX (602) 542-5680

DUANE BELCHER, SR.
CHAIRMAN

MEMBERS
KATHRYN D. BROWN
DONNA FLANIGAN
TOM FREESTONE
HOWARD JARRETT
EDWARD M. LEYVA
STAN F. TURLEY

July 2, 1996

Mr. Richard Rossi, ADOC# 50337
ASPCF-CB6
P.O. Box 8600
Florence, AZ 85232

Dear Mr. Rossi:

The Arizona Board of Executive Clemency has received a copy of the Warrant of Execution issued by the Supreme Court of the State of Arizona, setting July 24, 1996, as the date for your execution. The purpose of this letter is to inform you that the Board has scheduled a hearing for the purpose of considering a reprieve.

I have set the date of your Reprieve hearing for July 19, 1996, at 8:30 a.m. This hearing will be held in the Eyman Complex-Special Management Unit I at the Arizona State Prison in Florence, Arizona. At your request, a Commutation of Sentence hearing will also be held at this time.

In Arizona, only the Governor can grant a reprieve/commutation, but he is restricted from granting any executive clemency action unless it is first recommended to him by the Arizona Board of Executive Clemency.

Our records show Denise Young of Arizona Capital Representation as your attorney of record. A notice of this hearing is also being furnished to that office. If this has changed, please notify our office so that a notice of this hearing can be forwarded to your attorney. You may have your attorney and any witnesses present that you feel can provide the Board with relevant information. If your scheduled execution is stayed by any court prior to your hearing, please notify my office. The Board reserves the right to cancel or reschedule your hearing if the execution date is changed by any court order.

If you or your attorney needs any additional information, please do not hesitate to contact me.

Sincerely,

Duane Belcher, Sr.

Duane Belcher, Sr.
Chairman

DB/dk

cc: Denise Young, Attorney

Arizona Board of Executive Clemency: Clemency Attendance Form

JANE DEE HULL
GOVERNOR

Michael D. Garvey
EXECUTIVE DIRECTOR

EDWARD M. LEYVA
CHAIRMAN

MEMBERS
KATHRYN D. BROWN
H. JARRETT
STAN F. TURNLEY
DONNA FLANIGAN
DUANE BELCHER, SR.

Arizona
Board of Executive Clemency

1645 WEST JEFFERSON
SUITE 334
PHOENIX, ARIZONA 85007
(602) 542-5636
FAX: (602) 542-5410

DATE: ______________________

APPLICANT'S NAME: ______________ ADC# __________ DOB ________ AGE ____

COMMITTING OFFENSE(S) ____________ SENTENCE(S) ____________ COMMITTING COUNTY ____________

DETAINER: YES ____ NO ____ IF SO, WHAT JURISDICTION ______________________

STATE EXACTLY WHAT YOU ARE ASKING THE BOARD OF PARDONS AND PAROLES TO RECOMMEND TO THE GOVERNOR:

____

STATE DESCRIPTIONS:

- How has your behavior been since incarceration?

____

- What positive accomplishments have you achieved since imprisonment? That is, have you participated in available educational, vocational and therapeutic programs? Include a description of your work record since incarceration.

____

- why do you believe you are entitled to a change of sentence?

____

(Over)

CONTINUATION OF SENTENCE APPLICATION

STATE DESCRIPTIONS CONTINUED:

- Describe your involvement in the crime(s) for which you were sentenced.

- When released, what are your plans upon returning to society?

- Give any other information you believe the Board of Pardons and Paroles should consider.

Inmate Signature: ______________________ Date: ____________

Witness Signature: ______________________ Date: ____________

Witness Signature: ______________________ Date: ____________

DO NOT WRITE BELOW THIS LINE

CLEMENCY BOARD INFORMATION:

Date application was received by Board of Pardons and Paroles: ____________

Date applicant was certified eligible by the Department of Corrections: ____________

Date Phase I hearing held: ____________ Disposition: ____________

Date Phase II hearing held if passed: ____________ Disposition: ____________

MAIL THIS APPLICATION DIRECTLY TO:

ARIZONA DEPARTMENT OF CORRECTIONS
TIME COMPUTATION UNIT
1601 WEST JEFFERSON
PHOENIX, ARIZONA 85007

Form: 70501223

Arizona Board of Clemency: Clemency Request—Plea for Relief

JANE DEE HULL
GOVERNOR

EDWARD M. LEYVA
CHAIRMAN

Michael O. Garvey
EXECUTIVE DIRECTOR

MEMBERS
KATHRYN D. BROWN
H. JARRETT
STAN F. TURNLEY
DONNA FLANIGAN
DUANE BELCHER, SR.

Arizona
Board of Executive Clemency
1645 WEST JEFFERSON
SUITE 334
PHOENIX, ARIZONA 65007
(602) 542-5636
FAX: (602) 542-5410

DATE: __________

APPLICANT'S NAME:______________ ADC#________ DOB______ AGE

COMMITTING OFFENSE(S)__________ SENTENCE(S)____________ COMMITTING COUNTY____________

DETAINER: YES___ NO___ IF SO, WHAT JURISDICTION______________________________

STATE EXACTLY WHAT YOU ARE ASKING THE BOARD OF PARDONS AND PAROLES TO RECOMMEND TO THE GOVERNOR:

STATE DESCRIPTIONS:

+ How has your behavior been since incarceration?

+ What positive accomplishments have you achieved since imprisonment? That is, have you participated available educational, Vocational and therapeutic programs? Include a description of your work record since incarceration.

+ why do you believe you are entitled to a change of sentence?

(Over)

CONTINUATION OF SENTENCE APPLICATION

STATE DESCRIPTIONS CONTINUED:

+ Describe your involvement in the crime(s) for which you were sentenced.

+ When released, what are your plans upon returning to society?

+ Give any other information you believe the Board of Pardons and Paroles should consider.

Inmate Signature: Date:

Witness Signature: Date:

Witness Signature: Date:

DO NOT WRITE BELOW THIS LINE

CLEMENCY BOARD INFORMATION:

Date application was received by Board of Pardons and Paroles:

Date applicant was certified eligible by the Department of Corrections:
Date Phase I hearing held: ________ Disposition:
Date Phase II hearing held if passed: ______ Disposition:

MAIL THIS APPLICATION DIRECTLY TO:
ARIZONA DEPARTMENT OF CORRECTIONS
TIME COMPUTATION UNIT
1601 WEST JEFFERSON
PHOENIX, ARIZONA 85007

Form: 70501223

Execution Procedures

TABLE OF CONTENTS

Article Six

Execution Procedures

Management Order # 44- Public Access to ADC Policies

1

R5-1-601. Definitions

The following definitions shall apply for the purposes of this Article, unless the context specifies otherwise:

1. "Condemned Inmate." A person who has been convicted by a court of record and sentenced to the death penalty.
2. "Contraband." Any item that is considered to be a detriment to the safe or orderly operation of the institution, including, but not limited to:
   a. Any item that could be used as an aid to escape.
   b. Any item that could be used to disguise or alter the appearance of an inmate.
   c. Any item of clothing or items for personal use or consumption that are not cleared first through the property room of the institution.
   d. Cameras, video, audio or related equipment.
   e. Any item, the possession of which is a felony or misdemeanor.
3. "Department." The Arizona Department of Corrections.
4. "Inmate." A person who is convicted and committed to the Department by any court of record or who is confined therein under the provisions of any agreement or compact to which the state or the Department is a party.
5. "Non-Contact Visit." A visit between an inmate and a visitor that is conducted without any physical contact and with a physical barrier between them.
6. "Warden." The Senior Warden of the Arizona State Prison, Florence and Eyman Complexes, in Florence, Arizona, where executions are held, or a Warden or Deputy Warden, if designated by the Senior Warden.
7. "Witness." A person who is invited to be present at an execution of sentence of death in accordance with A.R.S. 13-706.

R5-1-602. Visitation restrictions for inmates segregated pending execution

A. A condemned inmate shall be segregated 14 days prior to the scheduled execution.

B. While the inmate is so segregated, Department staff shall closely observe the condemned inmate at all times, and the following visitation restrictions shall apply:

2

1. All visits shall be non-contact visits.

2. Visits shall be allowed by a licensed attorney who represents the condemned inmate on the conviction for which the inmate has been sentenced to death. A paralegal or investigator who is employed by, or an agent of, the attorney and who has written authorization signed by the attorney shall be allowed to visit on behalf of the attorney.

3. Other visitation shall be authorized only for:

   a. Those individuals who are listed on the condemned inmate's Visiting List, as defined in R5-1-101(13), at the time the death warrant is served. The visiting list shall not be changed after the death warrant is served.

   b. A person who is a Relative or Immediate Family member, as defined in R5-1-101(11) but who is not on the inmate's visiting list shall be allowed to visit;

   c. Clergy; and

   d. Special Visits as defined in R5-1-111, if authorized by the Warden.

C. The Warden may prohibit any person from visiting a condemned inmate, if the Warden determines that the visit could pose a serious threat to the life or physical safety of any individual or the safe, secure, or orderly operation of the prison.

D. Except for the restrictions on visitation in this article, Title 5, Chapter 1, Article 1 rules on visitation shall apply to visitors.

R5-1-603. Admission of witnesses

A. Each potential witness to an execution shall present an original invitation from the Director prior to admittance to the prison.

B. Each potential witness shall present acceptable verification of identification upon entering the prison.. This identification shall include a picture, name and date of birth. Examples of acceptable picture identification are:

1. Military identification card.
2. Passport.
3. Valid state drivers license.

4. An official picture identification card from any state or federal agency, including government employee identification cards, and Immigration and Naturalization documentation cards.

C. Each potential witness shall be subject to the following:

1. Inspection for contraband;

2. Clearing a metal detector;

3. A pat-down search; and

4. A strip search, if the Warden determines that there is a reasonable suspicion that a person is in possession of contraband that could pose a serious threat to the life or physical safety of any individual or the safe, secure and orderly operation of the prison. If the person refuses to be strip searched, the person shall be denied entry.

D. All items in the possession of a witness shall be subject to inspection.

R5-1-604. Items that may be brought into prisons

A witness may bring the following items into a prison:

1. Usual, customary and seasonal personal wearing apparel.

2. Personal identification.

3. Keys, wallets and purses.

4. One disposable lighter and one unopened package of cigarettes.

5. Prescription medication in the original container, and only in the amount needed during the period of time the witness may be expected to be inside the prison.

6. No more than two pens or pencils and one writing tablet, which is no larger than eight and one-half by eleven inches and contains no metal parts.

R5-1-605. Conduct of witnesses

A. A witness to an execution shall not be permitted to interview staff, inmates or other witnesses while inside the prison.

B. While inside the prison, no witness shall draw, sketch, paint or otherwise graphically depict, in any way any person, area or activity inside the prison during the execution.

C. A witness who does not comply with sections (A) and (B) above shall be escorted off prison grounds by

4

Department staff and shall not be allowed to witness the execution.

R5-1-606. Crowd control during executions.

A. The Warden shall assign areas on prison grounds for public assembly, vigils or demonstrations. Members of the public shall be directed to the designated areas.

B. Individuals who wish to assemble shall not bring items of contraband onto prison property.

C. Members of the public shall conduct themselves in accordance with any verbal directions given by Department staff and all written instructions or regulations posted on prison grounds.

D. No food or beverages may be brought onto prison grounds.

E. No noise-makers or items that can produce loud sounds shall be brought onto prison grounds.

F. Visitors on prison property are subject to the search provision of R5-1-603(D).

G. Visitors shall park only in designated areas.

H. Any person who violates any of the rules in this Article, or who is otherwise found by Department staff to be a threat to the health or safety of any person or to the safe, secure or orderly operation of the prison may be removed from prison grounds by Department staff.

5

Method of Execution

ARIZONA DEPARTMENT OF CORRECTIONS

METHOD OF EXECUTION

I,__________________________ have a scheduled execution date of
(Inmate Name)

_________________________________.
(Date)

CHECK ONE

[ ] LETHAL INJECTION

[ ] LETHAL GAS

I understand that I may request a change in this process no later than 20 days prior to my scheduled execution date, after which time no changes will be allowed. If I do not exercise a choice, the method of execution will be lethal injection.

__________________________ _______________
Inmate's Signature (Date)

__________________________ _______________
Staff Signature (Witness) (Date)

__________________________ _______________
Staff Signature (Witness) (Date)

Form: 70501148
Rev.: 12/15/94

Condemned Inmate Witness/Notification Information

ARIZONA DEPARTMENT OF CORRECTIONS

CONDEMNED INMATE WITNESS/NOTIFICATION INFORMATION

FROM	ADC#	DATE OF PREPARATION

I hereby request that the following actions be taken on my behalf relating to my forthcoming execution.

I. I request the witnesses listed below be invited:

Name	Relationship	Mailing Address	TELEPHONE Business	TELEPHONE Home

II. I request the below listed clergy be in attendance:

III. I request the below listed next-of-kin be notified of my death:

IV. My Attorney of Record is:

Inmate's Signature	Witness Signature and Title

Form: 70501150
Rev: 09/08/04

Disposition of Property

ARIZONA DEPARTMENT OF CORRECTIONS

DISPOSITION OF PROPERTY

I, ______________, have a scheduled execution date of ____________. Upon completion of my execution, I request that my property be released to ___________________________, who is not an inmate and who has agreed to distribute such property to the appropriate persons for disposition in accordance with the applicable State law.

___________________________ can be reached at the following location or in the following manner: ____.

I understand that, if I do not designate a person willing to accept my property as stated above, my property will be released in accordance with Departmental policy.

I further understand that, if the person(s) entitled to the release of my property, either through designation herein or in accordance with Departmental policy, do(es) not take possession of my property within 90 days after my execution, my property will be disposed of at the discretion of prison officials.

________________________________ ________________

Inmate's Signature Date

________________________________ ________________

Staff Signature (Witness) Date

________________________________ ________________

Staff Signature (Witness) Date

Form 40000184
Rev. 11/30/95

Disposition of Remains

ARIZONA DEPARTMENT OF CORRECTIONS

DISPOSITION OF REMAINS

(ARS § 36-381)

I, ______________________ have a scheduled execution date of ________________
(Name) (Date)

I understand that, upon completion of my execution, my body will be released to my surviving spouse, who will be responsible for my funeral and burial arrangements. If I have no surviving spouse or if my surviving spouse is not willing or financially able to provide for my burial and funeral arrangements, my body will be released to my adult children who will be responsible for my funeral and burial arrangements. If I have no surviving spouse and no surviving adult children, or if my surviving spouse or my surviving adult children are not willing or financially capable of providing for my burial and funeral arrangements, or if my surviving spouse or my surviving adult children cannot be located on reasonable inquiry, my body will be released to any person or fraternal charitable or religious organization willing to assume responsibility for my funeral and burial arrangements. If none of the above persons is willing or financially capable of providing for my funeral and burial arrangements, I understand that my body will be released to the Arizona Department of Corrections for burial in either a County indigent cemetery or at the ASPC-Florence/ Eyman cemetery located in Florence, Arizona.

In order to facilitate the disposition of my remains, I provide the following information (please check those items that are applicable to you and provide any required information):

☐ I do not have a surviving spouse.

☐ The name of my surviving spouse is ______________________ who may be reached at the following location or in the following manner: ______________
____

☐ I do not have any surviving adult children.

☐ The names of my surviving adult child(ren) is/are: ______________
____

They may be reached at the following location or in the following manner:
____
____
____

☐ In the event I have no surviving spouse and no surviving adult children, or if my surviving spouse or my surviving adult children are not willing or financially capable of providing for my burial and funeral arrangements, or if my surviving spouse or my surviving adult children cannot be located on reasonable inquiry, I request that my body be released to ______________________________ who is willing to assume responsibility for my burial and funeral arrangements and who can be reached at the following location or in the following manner:______________________________.
I understand that, if the person designated above is unwilling to assume responsibility for my burial and funeral arrangements, my body will then be released to any person or fraternal charitable or religious organization willing to assume responsibility for my burial and funeral arrangements. In the event that no such person or organization comes forward, my body will be released to and disposed of by officials of the Arizona Department of Corrections.

______________________________ ____________________
Inmate's Signature Date

______________________________ ____________________
Staff Witness Signature Date

______________________________ ____________________
Staff Witness Signature Date

Form 40000183
Rev. 11/30/95

Last Will and Testament

LAST WILL AND TESTAMENT OF

____
(Inmate Name)

I, _______________________________, a resident of _______________________________
(Inmate Name) (City)

_______________________, _______________________, make and publish this my Last Will and
(County) (State)

Testament.

I hereby declare that I am _______________________________. The names of my
(marital status, i.e. single, married, divorced, etc.)

closest blood relatives are: _______________________________

____

____

____

____

____

____

I request that upon my death/execution, my body be released to: _______________________

_______________________________ who will be responsible for funeral and

burial arrangements.

I nominate _______________________________, as executor/executrix of this my Last

Will and Testament.

I leave the following specific bequests:

Last Meal Request

ARIZONA DEPARTMENT OF CORRECTIONS
LAST MEAL REQUEST

MEMO FOR RECORD — **DATE:** ______________________
Month Day Year

TO: ASPC-F FOOD SERVICES

SUBJECT: LAST MEAL REQUEST

Due to the proximity of my execution date (______________________), I request that my
Month Day Year

last meal consist of the following items:

____

____

____

____

____

____

I understand that my last meal shall be reviewed in conjunction with food items which are readily available, either in the prison food inventory or which can be obtained locally from a grocery store. The quantity of food afforded to me shall be in reasonable portions that normally would be consumed at a meal and which could be eaten within a thirty minute time period.

This is my last and final meal request. I will not resubmit this request.

______________________ ______________________
Requestor's Signature **Witness's Signature**

Form: 70501222
09/17/91

Inmate Disciplinary Penalties and Violations

ATTACHMENT C
ADC Policy #103.3.1
INMATE DISCIPLINARY PENALTIES AND VIOLATIONS

DISCIPLINARY PENALTIES

The Disciplinary Hearing Officer may impose any or all penalties listed for that category according to the severity of the offense.

The Coordinator may only impose penalties as indicated in policy, but may not impose loss of earned release credits, placement in Parole Class III, placement in disciplinary detention or restitution.

Commission of three minor violations within a 90-day period may constitute a Group B major offense.

PENALTIES	GROUP A MAJOR	GROUP B EITHER MAJOR OR MINOR	GROUP C MINOR
DENTION	0 - 15 DAYS	0 - 10 DAYS	NO
TIME LOSS RECOMMENDATION	0 - ALL	AGGRAVATED - Up to 8 months STANDARD - up to 5 months MITIGATED - Up to 2 months	NO
PLACEMENT IN PAROLE CLASS III	0 - 90 days	0 - 60 days	NO
LOSS OF PRIVILEGES	YES	YES	YES
RESTITUTION	YES	YES	NO
EXTRA DUTY	YES	YES	YES
REPRIMAND	YES	YES	YES
RESTRICTION	YES	YES	YES

Attachment C
103.3.1
Page 2 Of 4

DISCIPLINARY VIOLATIONS

GROUP A VIOLATIONS

A01 Inciting or participating in a riot, disturbance, demonstration or work stoppage.

A02 Taking a hostage or kidnapping.

A03 Intentionally causing the death or great bodily injury of another person.

A04 Sexual assault.

A05 Assault or battery with a deadly weapon or any assault on staff.

A06 Escape, aiding escape or preventing the discovery of an escape.

A07 Arson.

A08 Negligence or carelessness causing death or great bodily injury.

A09 Possession or manufacture of dangerous contraband to include weapons, explosives, escape paraphernalia, tools, keys, currency, unauthorized identification or other official documents, civilian clothing or part of any official uniform or any other item not authorized, which is deemed a threat to the security of the institution.

A10 Conspiracy, attempt to commit or prevent the discovery of any group A violation.

GROUP B VIOLATIONS

B01 Assault, battery or striking any person with any weapon or object to include hands, fists or feet.

B02 Threatening any person with bodily harm.

B03 Fighting.

B04 Extortion or intimidation.

B05 Lying or presenting false or misleading information to staff, volunteers or others acting in official capacity.

B06 Tampering with any security or safety equipment.

Attachment C
103.3.1
Page 3 Of 4

GROUP B VIOLATIONS

B07 Possession, manufacture or consumption of, or trafficking in any drug, narcotic, intoxicant, stimulant, depressant, drug paraphernalia of unprescribed medicine.

B08 Disobeying a verbal or written order, including Departmental and institutional rules, policies, procedures, memoranda or other directives.

B09 Obstructing, hindering or impeding staff in the performance of their duties.

B10 Engaging in any sexual act, including indecent exposure and sexual advances or stalking of another person.

B11 Giving or receiving tattoos or possession of tattooing paraphernalia.

B12 Loss, destruction or damage of property.

B13 Theft or possession of stolen property.

B14 Giving or offering a bribe or anything of value to any staff member or other agent of the department.

B15 Fraud.

B16 Disrespect in the form of profanity, obscene or abusive language or gestures.

B17 Unauthorized physical contact.

B18 Counterfeiting or forging any official document or currency.

B19 Gambling or possession of gambling paraphernalia.

B20 Refusing to work, report to work or complete work assignment.

B21 Disorderly conduct.

B22 Interfering or disrupting count or failing to be present at the designated time and place for count.

B23 Violating or attempting to violate any of the laws of the state of Arizona or the United States of America.

B24 Smuggling or introduction into the institution of any contraband.

B25 Throwing or projecting an item at another person.

B26 Conspiracy or attempt to commit or prevent the discovery of any Group B Violation.

B27 Commission of three minor violations within a 90-day period.

Attachment C
103.3.1
Page 4 Of 4

GROUP C VIOLATIONS

C01 Possession of contraband items including excess clothing and linen, altered items considered contraband as defined by policy and not included in violation B-7.

C02 Horseplay

C03 Unauthorized altering of physical appearance.

C04 Bartering, selling or trading goods or services with other inmates.

C05 Feigning illness or malingering.

C06 Failure to maintain personal hygiene or appearance requirements.

C07 Failure to maintain sanitation or cleanliness requirements in the living, work or any area to which the inmate is assigned.

C08 Being in an unauthorized area, absence from assigned area or failure to report to an authorized area or destination.

C09 Littering.

C10 Use of machinery or equipment in an unauthorized or unsafe manner.

C11 Participating in an unauthorized meeting or gathering.

C12 Conspiracy or attempt to commit or prevent the discovery of any GROUP C violation.

Public Information Manual, Table of Contents

ARIZONA DEPARTMENT OF CORRECTIONS

TABLE OF CONTENTS

PUBLIC INFORMATION MANUAL

Management Order # 44
Public Access to ADC Policies

Arizona Department of Corrections: Latest News Release

Saturday May 8, 1999 P202

ARIZONA DEPARTMENT OF CORRECTIONS
1601 West Jefferson Street
Phoenix, Arizona 85007

News Releases

Latest News :

NEW *CORRECTIONAL OFFICERS WEEK: GOVERNOR ANNOUNCES PAY RAISE*

FORMER DEATH ROW INMATE SERIOUSLY ASSAULTED

INDICTMENT IN PARALEGAL SERVICES CASE

Warrant of Execution *Robert Wayne Vickers* , for May 5, 1999

NEW Warrant of Execution *Michael Kent Poland* . for June 16, 1999

Updated Friday, April 30, 1999 04:37:05 PR

Arizona State Prison Complex—Florence

Arizona State Prison Complex- Florence

Historical Information
Execution Information
ASPC-Florence Wardens
Gas Chamber
Death Row Information
Florence Cemetery

HISTORICAL INFORMATION

In the beginning, the Arizona State Prison at Florence consisted of two (2) housing wings (APocket@ and AWeed Row@), a TB Wing and the ASnakes@. The ASnakes@ was an underground cell area for solitary confinement. It was called ASnakes@ due to the fact that snakes would find their way into it. Inmates were transferred from Yuma Territorial prison to Florence in the late 1800's. The new prison was a distinct improvement over Yuma, however, the prison at Florence had a death chamber. In the beginning, the death chamber was located one floor above the cells on death row. The chamber itself was a scaffold and, in the floor, a trap door was constructed through which the bodies of the hanged fell into a room below. As you can see, the Florence Prison has changed since that time. The oldest buildings on-site include the Administration Building (built in 1928) and Cellblock Two (CB-2). Construction began on CB-2 in 1928 and it was completed in 1930. The gates leading into the Central Unit, of which CB-2 is part, were brought to Florence from the Yuma Territorial Prison.

In 1973, there was a riot/hostage situation in ASPC-F Central Unit. Two (2) staff were killed by inmates in Cellblock Three (CB-3). Before and since this time, there have been no incidents of staff fatalities within the secure perimeter of the Florence institutions. The Department continually reviews and enhances security to ensure the safety and security of the staff and inmates of the State of Arizona.

Within Central Unit, there is a tunnel which runs from CB-2 to the Administration Building. This tunnel was sealed in 1985 when it was discovered that inmates had found a way to access the tunnels. In addition, around this same time, the CB-2 tower was replaced. The existing tower was deteriorating and plans were made to utilize it as a control room. However, in 1985, the estimated cost for renovation and a locking system was approximately $4,000,000.00. Needless to say, this project was not initiated.

Usually of great interest to individuals visiting the Florence Prison is the Death House. Death sentences have been carried out in Florence since 1910. The first individual executed by hanging at Florence was Jose Lopez on January 5, 1910. From that time until July 7, 1916, eight (8) more individuals were executed. Effective December 8, 1916, an initiative measure passed which deleted the provision for the death penalty in Arizona. The death penalty was restored in December 5, 1918. Nineteen (19) executions by hanging occurred between April 16, 1920 and June 20, 1931.

The first execution by lethal gas was carried out when two (2) brothers, Manuel and Fred Hernandez, were executed at 5:00 a.m. on July 6, 1934. On March 4, 1962, Manuel E. Silvas was executed by lethal gas at 5:08 a.m. In 1972, the Arizona Supreme Court adopted a policy of reducing death sentences to life. In August 1973, the death penalty again was effective, however, in 1978, a ruling was made that the Arizona Statute regarding executions was unconstitutional and all executions were stayed. In 1979, the Arizona Legislature revised the Arizona Death Penalty Statute and Death Sentences again became effective May 1, 1979. On April 5, 1992 at 12:18 a.m., twenty-nine (29) years after the execution of Manuel Silvas, Donald E. Harding was put to death by lethal gas.

In November 1992, Arizona voters approved execution by lethal injection. By law, any person sentenced to death prior to November 23, 1992 is afforded a choice of execution by either lethal gas or lethal injection. Inmates receiving a death sentence after November 23, 1992 are executed by lethal injection.

Walter B. LaGrand was the last prisoner to be executed by lethal gas on March 3, 1999. Since the implementation of lethal injection, fourteen (14) inmates have been executed utilizing this method. Because we still have inmates who received a death sentence prior to January 1993, the gas chamber is maintained in working order in the event an individual chooses this method of execution.

Additional historical information regarding the Florence Prison is available in the Town of Florence at the local Pinal County Historical Society Museum. Original inmate registration record books dating back to the late 1800's, the first lethal gas chair and ropes utilized in hanging executions are only a small sample of items on exhibit. The Pinal County Historical Society Museum is located at:

715 South Main Street
Florence, Arizona 85232
(520) 868-4382

EXECUTION INFORMATION

At this time, all Death Row inmates, with the exception of two (2) women on Death Row in the Phoenix Perryville facility, are housed at the Eyman Complex in Florence within the Special Management Unit II (SMU II). There are approximately 120 inmates under sentences of death in Arizona. Death sentences are carried out at the Arizona State Prison Complex at Florence (ASPC-F).

When an inmate receives a Warrant of Execution, a schedule is developed for submission of related forms and inmate movement. Inmates under a Warrant of Execution remain at SMU II until 48 to 24 hours prior to their scheduled execution. At that time, affected inmates are transferred to Death House within Central Unit of ASPC-F.

One (1) pound of sodium-cyanide is placed in a container underneath the gas chamber chair. The chair is made of perforated metal which allows the cyanide gas to pass through and fill the chamber. A bowl below the gas chamber contains sulfuric acid and distilled water. A lever is pulled and the sodium-cyanide falls into the solution, releasing the gas. It takes the prisoner several minutes to die. After the execution, the excess gas is released through an exhaust pipe which extends about 50 feet above Death House.

Inmates executed by lethal injection are brought into the injection room a few minutes prior to the appointed time of execution. He/she is then strapped to a Gurney-type bed and two (2) sets of intravenous tubes are inserted - one (1) in each arm. The three (3) drugs utilized include: Sodium Pentothal (a sedative intended to put the inmate to sleep), Pavulon (stops breathing and paralyzes the muscular system) and Potassium Chloride (causes the heart to stop). Death by lethal injection is not painful and the inmate goes to sleep prior to the fatal effects of the Pavulon and Potassium Chloride.

FURTHER INFORMATION

The writings of Richard Michael Rossi: www.richie-rossi.com

To contact Richard Michael Rossi directly:

Richard Michael Rossi #50337
ASPC-Eyman-SMU2
P.O. Box 3400
Florence, AZ 85232
USA

Arizona Department of Corrections: www.adc.state.az.us

Death Penalty Information Center: www.deathpenaltyinfo.org

Cell Door Magazine: www.celldoor.com

Inside/Outside: www.home.planet.nl/~inside-outside

Canadian Coalition Against the Death Penalty: www.ccadp.org

Abolition France: www.abolition.fr.vu

Crime and Punishment: www.crimeandpunishment.org

LifeLines: www.lifelines.org

Amnesty International: www.amnesty.org

Reprieve: www.reprieve.org

About the Author

Richard Michael Rossi was born and raised in Brooklyn, New York. He graduated from Pace College in 1970 with a Bachelor's degree in Accounting and Business Administration. He went on to work as an accountant and was successful in various businesses. Personal tragedies resulted in his resorting to drugs to overcome the pain in his life. He became addicted to cocaine and amphetamines. While living in Phoenix, Arizona, he committed a murder while trying to obtain money for more drugs. He was tried and convicted of first degree murder and sentenced to death.

For over 20 years he has been on Arizona's death row. During this time he became a paralegal and then he became the prison library clerk. He turned to writing about the death penalty and about conditions on death row. His articles, essays, and poems have been published in the abolitionist community across America and around the world. He has worked and continues to work with abolitionists in an attempt to help eliminate the death penalty by enlightening those in the free world about the real life of death row prisoners in America.

He was encouraged to write a book about the death penalty and conditions on death row. He wrote this book, *Waiting to Die: Life on Death Row*, while facing his last appeal.